"*Existential Social Work: Making Meaning in the Face of Distress* provides an innovative approach to therapeutic practice. Analyzing practice from a philosophical perspective that is accessible to readers, the book offers practitioners and students a creative way for understanding and addressing the problems of their clients."

Stanley L Witkin, *expert in social constructivist theory in social work; President, GPTSW; former editor-in-chief of Social Work; Professor Emeritus of Social Work, University of Vermont; Adjunct Professor, University of Pennsylvania*

"*Existential Social Work: Making Meaning in the Face of Distress* weaves together existential theory with practice wisdom and a reflective stance, to describe and analyze the therapeutic process of reconstructing meaning. As such this book is bound to become an important resource for both scholars and practitioners interested in the field."

Zahava Solomon, *Professor Emerita, Bob Shapell School of Social Work; eminent trauma researcher; Head of The Multidisciplinary Center of Excellence for Mass Trauma Research, Tel Aviv University; holder of the Israel Price for Excellence in Social Sciences*

Existential Social Work

This book is a theoretical and practical guide for mental health professionals who wish to utilize existential principles in their social work and clinical practice.

Existential questions concerning life situations, such as anxiety, suffering, choosing, authenticity, are at the heart of the craft of any helping profession. The book aims to confront students and practitioners with the need to be simultaneously philosophical and experiential in their clinical approach. Written in an accessible tone, Eisikovits and Buchbinder bridge existential-philosophical concepts often seen as removed from everyday practice and the practical concerns of therapy. Each chapter presents a concept from existential philosophical tradition, such as anxiety, meaning making, time, and space, and then demonstrates their use by drawing from real-life clinical examples and interventions.

The book illustrates their implementation in social work practice with reference to values such as client participation, self-determination, and free will. The book is intended for courses and advanced training in existential social work and therapy. It is essential reading for training social workers, counselors, therapists, and other helping professionals interested in existentialism.

Zvi Eisikovits, PhD, is Professor Emeritus of social welfare and criminology, former Dean of the Faculty of Welfare and Health Studies at the University of Haifa in Israel, and former director of the Center for the Study of Society. He has published around 120 articles and four books, mostly on the topics of intimate partner violence, elder abuse, and existentialism in practice.

Eli Buchbinder, PhD, is an associate professor at the School of Social Work, University of Haifa, Israel. He specializes in qualitative research and has published numerous journal articles in various fields of practice using existential theory. He has extensive experience as a social worker in various capacities.

Existential Social Work

Meaning Making in the Face
of Distress

Zvi Eisikovits and Eli Buchbinder

Routledge
Taylor & Francis Group

NEW YORK AND LONDON

Designed cover image: Artwork by Maayan Harel

First published 2023
by Routledge
605 Third Avenue, New York, NY 10158

and by Routledge
4 Park Square, Milton Park, Abingdon, Oxon, OX14 4RN

Routledge is an imprint of the Taylor & Francis Group, an informa business

ISBN: 9781032344249 (hbk)
ISBN: 9781032344232 (pbk)
ISBN: 9781003322085 (ebk)

DOI: 10.4324/9781003322085

Typeset in Sabon
by Apex CoVantage, LLC

I dedicate the book to my wife Rivka, my son Nir and daughter-in-law Masha, and my granddaughters Naomi and Nina who each made my life meaningful in their unique ways, Zvi

I dedicate the book to my wife Goldi (Golda) and my daughter Lotem, who made my existence meaningful, Eli

Contents

Acknowledgments

We wrote this book after a lengthy learning and reflection process from our teachers in social work and existential philosophy. We thank them for showing us the light and participating in the initiation process. Our best teachers were our students and clients who asked questions and argued with us in a truly Talmudic fashion, illuminating the advantages of multiple realities and challenging viewpoints. This book would have never been written without the kind support of Heather Evans, Commissioning Editor at Taylor & Francis Group whose promoting enthusiasm made it all come true. Beyond her knowledge and professional competence, she made us feel along the way that we have a sensitive and caring alliance. We also thank Dr Gabriel Lanyi who was not only a professional editor but a friend and a consultant in closing the gap between what we meant and what we wrote. We thank Mayan Harrel, the talented graphic artist, for the creative cover expressing the search underlying this book. We finally acknowledge the University of Haifa Research Authority for being our safe nest, encouraging us in our work and supporting us morally and financially.

Prologue
Why existentialism? A roadmap

"Il faut imaginer Sisyphe heureux." This simple French sentence by Camus does not translate quite easily into English, but a close approximation would be "We must imagine that Sisyphus is happy." Happiness is not what we would associate with Sisyphus, the mythological hero punished (for cheating death, of all things) to forever drag a boulder uphill, only to have it roll down each time before reaching the top. This does not seem to be a recipe for happiness, but somehow, in Camus' view, Sisyphus manages to snatch contentment from the jaws of ordeal by endowing his absurd and thankless task with meaning—his own meaning. We are in the territory of existentialism, although Camus staunchly denied being a votary, preferring to talk about absurdism. But this is just a terminological quibble: the two are the obverse of one another (existentialism is the answer to the absurdity of being). Camus asked the great existential questions about whether and how to live, and about the meaning of existence, and concluding that the absurd universe was silent, he sought that answer within. On his way down the hill to resume his endless toil, Sisyphus seeks purpose in his defiance of the punishment, or perhaps in the perverse pleasure of the useless labor itself, like Solzhenitsyn's convicts in the Gulag, or like Dostoevsky's underground man, who seeks purpose in despair and hopelessness. And since we have no predetermined purpose (we are existentialists, after all), we can write our own script, which is what Sisyphus does to face despair and the absurdity of existence.

Our tasks, as individuals and social workers, may not be as daunting or senseless as that of Sisyphus, but it often requires all our internal resources to endow them with meaning. This book is about how existential thinking can help us in being and doing social work.

In the absence of a dominant paradigm or meta-narrative, we are faced with perpetually changing and emerging personal and social situations, in which change is the only constant, and we are expected to develop a backbone of endless flexibility. The quality and rhythm of change affect the overall structure of the social and psychological world through such processes as globalization, rising life expectancy, and changes in power,

DOI: 10.4324/9781003322085-1

in family relations and structure, in the position of marginalized and minority groups such as women, children, people with different sexual orientation, elderly people, persons with disability, and so on. Stability is replaced by transition, security by expectation. The inability to see ahead further adds to the constant tension and emergence where the meaninglessness and the search for meaning become givens. Existential philosophy and its implementation in therapy can serve as a reliable compass for navigating this sea of uncertainty without being deterred by meaninglessness. Existential thinking rejects the reductionist idea of linear causality and the homogenization of being. The aim is to provide a theoretical path for individuality and authenticity.

The theoretical is personal

Based on our knowledge of social work practitioners, we believe that the way to suggest the existential approach to social work novices as a practice theory is to emphasize personal commitment. To think existentially is to live existentially. Existentialism provides a solid ground for reflection and action on basic life issues, including suffering, meaning, responsibility, choice, authenticity, relationships with others, and more. Being existential demands not only developing, but also implementing existential attitudes in our own personal and professional life. Cox (2009) wrote that "A person can know about existentialism and be convinced of its truth, but they are not true existentialists if they make no effort to live the life" (p. 9). The existential approach imposes authenticity as part and parcel of being an existentialist professional.

Existentialists face the human condition directly

We are thrown into the world without a master plan to provide directions regarding what to do when. Cox (2009), again: "Existentialism is a fiercely honest philosophy that confronts human life for what it really is, building its comprehensive, holistic thesis based on certain undeniable facts or truths of the human condition, such as the truth that everyone is mortal, for example" (p. 8). To face the human condition is to experience existential anxiety arising from focusing on dealing with life's troubles, uncertainties, inconsistencies, and suffering. All of these are seen as inherent characteristics of being human. Yalom's (1980) conceptualization of the previous as "four ultimate concerns"—death, freedom, existential isolation, and meaninglessness—summarizes the human experience from this perspective.

Only face-to-face, direct preoccupation with the basics of existence produces anxiety that we must confront and use as a basis for change (May, 1983). Because of its preoccupation with death, existentialism tended to be presented as "the dark side of life," an overly negative philosophy. But in reality, existentialism suggests that encountering our finiteness may cause us to evaluate the authenticity of our mode of living and lead to more active choices concerning our present existence (May, 1958).

The existential attitude, as suggested by van Deurzen-Smith (1997), emphasizes that "The objective is to enable people to stand courageously in the tensions of life in a way that enables and revitalizes them, whilst taking account of the context and horizons of the world in which they live" (p. 3). Existentialism expects us to be aware of our finite options and yet live courageously.

Existential therapy has often been criticized as too complicated, too philosophical, far-fetched, and distant from social work clients' experiences. In our view and experience, existentialism perceives individuals as yearning for a deeper understanding of their being and searching for meaning and purpose in their life. This holds whether a person is poor or wealthy. We believe that the social worker has a professional obligation to capture the clients' everyday world and situation as they live it. There is no prescribed interpretation of what clients do or say. Rather, the worker needs to examine sensitively the applicability of the existential concepts and principles. The key helping tool in the process is language. The therapist should not view the encounter as a space filled with abstract language or terminology, or try to educate the client to use such language. Rather, the therapist should make the philosophical ideas suggested in this book concrete and adapt them to individual designs and situations. Being poor, criminal, or addicted is a descriptive fact that can be given meaning by the worker together with the client. Under no condition are the client's choices denied or minimized because of external considerations (e.g., poor people are less likely to construct meaning than the affluent are). For the social worker, this is an ethical obligation and as such, it is beyond question.

Meaning making

Existentialism endeavors to center one's being on seeking and creating meaning (Krill, 1996). As existentialist social workers, we aim to answer the toughest existential questions: What are we? What do we want out of life? What do we want to become? What is the meaning of anxiety and how do we experience it? How do we construct our attitude toward suffering? What to do with freedom? What do interactions with others mean to us? What do we project into the future and how? What responsibilities are inherent in our being? As we illustrated previously we are dealing with "what?" rather than "why?" questions. These questions converge into the broader concept of meaning in action. We should not assume that meanings are given and remain permanent. In the face of life events and constant changes, we must be aware of meaning and examine it on an ongoing basis. We encourage ourselves and our clients to provide satisfactory answers in the process of the foregoing inquiries, and we expect clients to be able to reflect on ways they plan to meet challenges and threats that will arise in the future.

The theory of existential practice is an active way of reflecting and coping by examining the narratives by which meaning is constructed. As professionals, we encourage building meaningful goals and values for life that can measure up with inevitable suffering and death.

In constructing meaning, existential social work requires workers to be open to the clients' situated and unique experiences, and to accept the subjectivity of the individual as the basis for understanding existence through meaning construction. This requires social workers to challenge ready-made recipes and theories concerning issues raised by clients. Existentialism reminds us that there are no easy solutions: meaning making is an ongoing struggle in the face of life changes and difficulties.

From here to the future

The critical time in existential thinking is the future. The future shapes life narratives as well as the thoughts, feelings, and acts related to the future orientation. Thus, existentialism focuses on the immediate experience of the here and now, as a projection into the future and reconstruction of past meaning according to it. This is somewhat counterintuitive, as we are used to thinking about the past as the origin and grounds for the future and as the justification for things as they are. Existentialists maintain that healing the wounds caused by negative experiences in the past is through meaning making for the future. The question that guides existential social work is not what happened and why, but what do I want to happen and what do I want to do about it? In other words, how will the constructed future help provide better solutions to life's ultimate concerns? Existential social work emphasizes what we do, including the minutest acts, as steppingstones in building meaning, from a position of commitment to choices.

Being in space

Together with time and the others, space is an essential ontological dimension of existence. It concretely signals the location where life events take place and narratives are constructed. It is also symbolic, representing existential meaning. For instance, home is both a location and a symbol of belonging. The answer to the question of who I am in the various spaces I occupy, in the past, present, and in future, uniquely identifies everyone. The answers that individuals provide are usually metaphoric. This is experienced as a journey and a search of one's path, overcoming obstacles leading to continuity, unity, meaning, and directionality toward being. Another special metaphoric use of space is applying social spaces to existence, for example, describing marriage as a prison or representing life experiences as a school. There is an ongoing dialectic between space, time, and others. The experience of a lack of horizon may create time-related distress. The experience of others may be one of closeness or distance, while the body is a key axis for the experience of space. This is particularly evident in situations of illness, when the body becomes central in experiencing the self and others.

Choosing freely

Existentialists perceive that what makes us humans different from other beings is the fact that we are free to choose what to do and what to be (Sartre, 1943/1966, 1946/1948; Thompson, 2017). Individuals do not exist as essences but are always becoming. Therefore, our interventions resist the image of the individual as passive in the face of deterministic causality, whether psychic or social. The image of the individual in any life situation is the result of self-creation. Our ability to choose freely makes us the authors of our lives. To be clear, existentialism does not claim that we are free in the sense of having no limits, that we control everything, or that we can be anything we set our mind to. It rather maintains that no matter what our condition or biography is, we embody freedom in our positions and choices. The only thing we are not free to choose is not to be free, or to use Sartre's words, we are condemned to be free. We cannot choose life circumstances, but we can choose our attitudes and responses to them. Although in many social work situations the expectation to exercise such choice is demanding and often impossible, it can be operationalized from an empathic position as an existential necessity. We recognize that people have the best reasons not to act upon their freedom to choose, but we are aware that this is the only empowering path to creating and recreating meaning. Therefore, existential intervention focuses on seeking meaning (Krill, 1996).

Individuals define and redefine themselves through choices (Cohn, 1997). When helping clients, we confine our intervention to changing their responses to unexpected circumstances, and conditions we do not choose and cannot control, summarized in the concept of thrownness. We position the freedom to choose as a dictum in the client's life. As social workers, we are at the epicenter of human dramas, recognizing that such freedom is a blessing and a curse, at the same time terrifying and exhilarating, and a creative force for growth (May, 1983).

The following case example encapsulates the complexities involved in freedom, choice, anxiety, and the interaction between them.

Monday around noon, Michelle, a married woman in her 30s, was driving from her residence in a small town to pick up her young son (one of her three children) from his kindergarten in a nearby town. It was raining. As she stopped at an intersection, a young boy and his friend, waiting by the side of the road, approached the car, opened the door, and asked where she was going. He asked her to take him and his friend, as they needed to get to the same place to visit a friend. Michelle felt bad about the youths getting wet and let them in. She had no suspicion about them, but at some point, she saw one of the youths hold a knife and felt the touch of the metal on her neck. She described later the sheer terror of death she experienced. She recalls that the youth ordered her to get off the road. She sought to delay this, driving with one hand to avoid and holding strong with the other the youngster's hand with the knife. She was able to bring the car to a sudden halt, knocked away the hand holding the knife, released her safety belt, and jumped out of the car, running for her life. Both youths escaped from the car. Michelle called the police and they were both arrested on the same day, and subsequently brought to trial. Michelle described the sense of "being thrown" into a life-threatening situation that traumatized her entire day-to-day experience from then on. She felt like a passive object, threatened with loss of her autonomy, helpless, and losing control over her life. Her basic need to regain control and safety became a daily preoccupation, permeating her family life. She described the lack of sensitivity and empathy of her partner, who had initially expressed anger over her anxious reaction. He expected "to move on, forget the whole thing and go on with life." Michelle described how her partner took some time to understand that she cannot put aside "the event," which became central in her experience. A further "sense of thrownness" developed when the probation services called to ask her to participate in a restorative justice process with the youths, under the professional supervision of social workers. Michelle was deeply conflicted about whether or not to take part in the process. The dilemma was the result of the fear to confront the perpetrators and re-experience the helplessness and lack of control associated with the situation that would be discussed. She wanted to know more about the process. In the preparatory stage that followed, the social worker held individual and family sessions with Michelle. It took about nine months until she felt safe enough to agree to continue the process. Throughout this preparation, she came to the recognition that choosing to join the process reflected her freedom to develop a position toward the event, its consequences, the perpetrators, and the threat of death. She realized that the process of restorative justice was an existential opportunity for her to face the question of the essence of human existence. She realized that she owed it to herself and her family to answer the basic question of whom she wanted to be. By doing so, she felt that she could build a more resilient life narrative.

Being responsible

It follows then that existentialism aims to transcend the experience of being trapped in anxiety arising from givens of life, to experience anxiety as a potential challenge and a possibility to construct meaning. This can be achieved only from a position of assuming responsibility. All humans are responsible for their becoming. Griffiths (2017) wrote that "Existential social work acknowledges the oppressive circumstances of clients' lives and how this shapes and determines their decision making and coping abilities. It aims to strengthen their abilities to grow, despite this oppression, and helps them take responsibility for shaping their own lives" (p. 22).

The human tendency is to oppose and deny freedom. There is an unwillingness to live up to it. Many flee in panic to safe havens, such as conventional beliefs, that limit their freedom. Responsibility requires confronting the tendency of individuals to ignore their freedom and distance themselves from it on an ongoing basis. We can be empathic without accepting excuses. The difficulty lies in the simultaneous acknowledgment of social and interpersonal oppression, and the need to avoid transforming it into an exemption from freedom, choice, and responsibility.

Responsibility is further involved with existential guilt. It is the inevitable result of having to choose from a myriad of options and to face the known and unknown consequences of choice. We need to accept our inability to foresee the future and the absence of guarantees. What we are left with are anxiety, meaning, and responsibility.

The dialectics of relational being and authenticity

Thinking existentially is thinking dialectically and aiming to integrate the extremes. Three main assumptions underlie such thinking: first is a contradiction, asserting the negation between opposing forces or polarities; second is unity and totality, viewing opposites as coexisting within a whole in a way that cannot be explained based on the nature of the constituent parts; and third, opposites remain bound to each other, never fully reconciled, creating tension, new understandings, and transformations.

A basic mission in existential social work is to integrate the dialectics in the relationship between self and others. Ontologically speaking, we are relational: the responsibility toward the world includes mostly others, but also our own values, ideas, roles, and more. At the other pole, we demand from ourselves to strive for authenticity. When it comes to intervention, being an existentialist social worker means striving toward an "authentic" action of both the client and the worker. Authenticity involves helping others cope and often revolt against outside pressures aimed at suppressing one's realness. It means being less self-deceiving, more decisive, more committed, and more willing to take on responsibility for the world (Thompson, 2017). In social work intervention, the ideal is to encourage better social functioning and to struggle against negative expectations and stigmas, together with the tendency to conform. Being authentic also means being ready to challenge the *status quo* of the social order at the individual and social levels, and to fight for social change (Griffiths, 2017). The responsibility for the self and others often creates conflicts. The challenge is to achieve a balance between these extremes.

Rabbi Menachem Mendel of Kotzk (1787–1859), a renowned Torah sage, and Hassidic master, said: "There is nothing more whole than a broken heart." In the previous context, we take this aphorism to mean that the effort required to create authenticity with respect to the self and others, even if resulting from the struggle to make whole the broken parts, is deeper and more coherent when the effort comes from the heart.

A warning is in order at this point: the number of approaches to existentialism is equal to the number of existentialist writers. It goes without saying that this is our version of it, but there seems to be a high level of agreement on several themes in existentialism, which, taken together, are within the realm of social work theory.

Thompson (2017) described the characteristics of existentialist practice as coherent with the mission of social work. He included reflective critical practice; a holistic approach that integrates the various aspects of a situation; a dialectical perspective involving the inter-relations of processes, both conflict and change; a demand for a clear and focused statement about the what and the how of intervention; partnership-oriented relationships in working with clients; empowering social workers to help clients achieve control through choices; practices focused on meaning; a view of reality as constructed through personal, cultural, and structural processes; assuming uncertainty; and emphasis on becoming.

Summary

The existential approach is a theoretical framework to be used as a GPS and compass in our intervention. The GPS and compass metaphor symbolizes the heuristic power arising from the mapping and direction-pointing capabilities of the concepts suggested. The first existential need arising from the theory is the need to reflect on issues that are not easy to live with. We, as social workers, are expected to be always involved in a process of confronting the realities of life vis-a-vis existential principles. We should remember that reality is not just out there, but rather constructed and reconstructed, and that it is our responsibility to determine how we construct and reconstruct it. This alone creates much insecurity and anxiety. Thus, to live and work existentially involves exacting challenges, chances to fail, and facing inherent ontological anxiety. Attempts to escape these experiences, to cast aside the burden, are the inducements of self-deception. Such attitudes are manifest in perceptions of lack of freedom, inability to make decisions, a sense of the absurd arising from the absence of meaning, denial of the value of authenticity, and avoidance of responsibility to connect with others and the world.

Having created a healthy amount of despair, we must note that attempts to act on existential principles in life situations and professional interventions result in a mixture of difficulty and vitality. The difficulty increases the sense of vitality. The questions related to basic concepts of freedom, choice, meaning, and responsibility leave little space for living a humdrum life. The expectation to set aside the taken-for-grantedness of life points toward the need to make a commitment involving a deeper level of being. We believe this book will provide readers with hope and encouragement to find a path to existentialism.

1 Anxiety

Being in the world

The term *Dasein* (Heidegger, 1927/1996), or human existence, meaning "being in the world," refers to the meaningful relational structures of being (Boss, 1963). Heidegger distinguished between two dimensions of Dasein: ontic and ontological (Cohn, 1997). The ontic dimension reflects the intrinsic aspects of being, which are given and unescapable. We are forced to be born into the world ("thrownness"), we must grow old, we must live, knowing and expecting death, and we must take a stand toward the freedom and limitations we have chosen. We can regard the ontological as the interpretive aspect of the entity, which gives meaning to the concrete being. The ontological dimension is unique to the Dasein in raising questions about its place in the world (Reynolds, 2006). Human beings perceive, experience, organize their existence, and act in a unique fashion evident in critical questions such as: Why am I here? What is important to me in this world? Why do these things happen to me? What should I do with my life and why does it matter? How free am I and what am I to do with what is unachievable? To whom am I indebted, what matters, and why? And naturally, Why live at all? By using the term "being in the world" we assume our situatedness in a context composed of people, ideas, and events that are interconnected in an inseparable whole (Iacovou & Weixel-Dixon, 2015). When we search for answers to these questions, Dasein becomes the subject of self-investigation. It relates to our ability to reflect on the meanings of experiences and life events, feelings, thoughts, values, expectations, ideals, and so on.

The process of asking and reflecting on being in the world is demanding and troubling. At times, it can bring individuals face-to-face with unclear, difficult, and unanswerable questions. In the process, individuals discover that they are lonely creators. In such dynamics, people escape from existential questions and challenges into ontic concerns. The ontic dimension is related to the concrete existence of entities. Humans prefer

DOI: 10.4324/9781003322085-2

to experience and stay at the everyday, concrete level. We perceive ourselves and others reflected in specific ways and acts. The ongoing basic existential situation is the outcome of relationships and meanings derived from epiphanic experiences that have the power to shape existence. Our world is always relational. As such, there are dialectical dynamics between the ontic and the ontological. We are existentially involved in the world through the everydayness of life. The following brief vignette is an illustration of this process:

> Monica is a 60-year-old woman. She is coping with the illness of her partner who was diagnosed with Alzheimer's disease. She approached the gerontological social worker and sought help to overcome the anger, disappointment, and helplessness that she felt toward her husband. Throughout the discussions, she expressed the sense that her entire reality betrayed her. Her friends aged and some died, others became cognitively challenged, still others were busy with their own difficulties. In addition, her married daughter moved away to a remote location. In the therapeutic sessions, the recurring life motif of overall control over her life resurfaced. Although she usually experienced control, recent life events eroded this feeling and led to loss of control and an overall sense of not finding herself. It became apparent that Monica's reflection was disturbed by turmoil arising from everyday relational experiences that filled her life (husband's illness, the passing and deterioration of friends, and the sense of loneliness arising from her daughter's move). Such epiphanic experiences create an ontic gap between the everyday control over reality and the sense that she was unable to actualize it.

Being has no constant essence but is part and parcel of mutual relationships. We must assume that understanding the meaning of the experience is to realize that it is co-constituted; therefore we must comprehend how individuals have structured their world (context) to give a relevant and applicable interpretation of how that experience is created (May, 1958). The structure and the relationship are the key dimensions of that which affirms being in the world (self-affirmation).

Our life events are fluid and change dynamically according to circumstances, other life events, losses, change, and more. One of the most profound experiences is the recognition of the limits of control we have over our lives. We must face the fact that certain aspects of our existence we simply cannot change: it starts with our genes, race, and family of origin, and continues with the history of our life and our environment. All these we must integrate into our Dasein (Heidegger, 1927/1997; Sartre,

1943/1966). Facts of life and constant changes create a dialectic between the ontic and the ontological. You cannot understand the ontic without the ontological or the other way around.

The state of thrownness, characteristic of the Dasein, reflects the nature of life. Overall, we must bridge between the ontic and the ontological. In many life situations, the movement between the ontic and the ontological is unclear, conflictual, and causes suffering. This dialectic is experienced as threatening and is a source of existential insecurity. Therefore, anxiety is at the heart of existence, it is inevitable, and therefore it is one of its critical pillars.

Anxiety—the beating heart of existence

May (1958, 1979) defined anxiety as the threat to the basis of our existence (a threat of imminent non-being) or to values underlying it. The experience of anxiety occurs when people feel the threat of not being able to affirm, reach, or preserve their goals and confirm their values, meanings, or future projects. Heidegger (1927/1996) maintained that anxiety is the collapse of everyday significance, and the result is a feeling of uncanniness. Anxiety is the subjective awareness that individuals can lose themselves and become nothing. It can be perceived metaphorically as the compass for our being in the world pointing toward the self, others, and the environment at large. In such challenging life situations, people may experience anguish, confusion, loss, paralysis, fury, and other negative emotions that color their being in the world. But as Spinelli (2007) wrote, experiences of anxiety "can re-awaken or enhance our connectedness to being alive and arouse creatively—*but only so long as such experiences permit the reshaping and reconstructing of a novel meaning that can be accepted and 'owned'*" (p. 28). Failure to do so results in a pervasive threat arising from the overall human condition rather than merely from an isolated part of oneself. The experience of anxiety is painful and potentially destructive. Fischer (1970) maintained that in anxious situations the focus is on "an ambiguous and contradictory state of affairs . . . signifying the problematic uncertainty of at least one of the projects upon which their respective self-understandings are founded" (p. 135). Such situations threaten the perception of the future. Angst is the result of feelings of panic, agitation, or dread about the nature of individual or human existence, beyond any specific event.

Existential distress may include concerns related to hopelessness, futility, meaninglessness, disappointment, remorse, death anxiety, and a disruption of personal identity. To be anxious is not knowing the cause of the dread (Vetlesen, 2009). "Angst," the German version of "anxiety," is the result of the Dasein experiencing itself as it is realized through possibilities once chosen by itself. Angst reveals Dasein as being possible. It expects the self to reflect on its existence and become aware of the potential of its being in the world. Cooper (1990) wrote that "*Angst* is the disturbing and 'uncanny' mood which summons a person to reflect on his individual existence and its 'possibilities'" (p. 128).

In contrast to fear, angst has no object. In the case of fear, one can take definitive measures to remove the object of fear, but in the case of angst, no such constructive measures are possible. This kind of anxiety is disconnected from the concrete circumstances of life, fears, and worries, yet at the same time, it is focused on the life circumstances. The dominant experience in such situations is one of nothingness. The use of the word "nothingness" in this context has to do both with the inherent insecurity about the consequences of one's actions, and with the fact that in experiencing freedom as angst, one also realizes that one is fully responsible for these consequences. Heidegger (1927/1996) maintained that existence itself is a source of anxiety for individuals, to remind them of the struggle with basic existential issues for which humans have no solutions. The concretization of the concept of nothingness is illustrated by Keren's experience of intimate partner violence for twenty years. Keren was referred to the social worker by police, after her husband's arrest following a complaint by a neighbor who feared for her and her child's safety. When asked why she did not complain all these years, including about this last event, Keren said that "all her life is destiny, and she was born to undergo this process." She further noted that she finds her inner calm in religion. She believed that there was no need for her to stop the suffering because God is watching and he'll stop it in due time. At the beginning of their relationship, the social worker failed to persuade her to complain to the police following threats and harassment by her husband from his place of arrest. After the social worker insisted, Keren complained, and the harassment stopped. Throughout the process, the prison social services informed Keren that her husband was transferred to a harsher facility where there was greater control over his communication with the outside world. This information created much fear and conflict in Keren because she did not want to initiate changes in his life. At the same time, the social worker sensed that Keren's ability to choose and act to defend herself and her child frightened her and created anxiety. Keren's meaning was embedded in destiny and God. If she acted on the threat and perceived herself to be in control of creating meaning, she would face nothingness, which in turn would create more anxiety and unveil the meaninglessness of her actions against her partner's violence.

Being in stark contrast with everything that defines existence and not knowing what anxiety is about makes people bewildered and unaware of what they feel. [Are people in stark contrast with everything that defines existence?] They become uncertain, powerless, and help-less about how to confront anxiety and make choices in the present about the future. Anxiety cancels meaning and forces an alien experi-ence of reality on us (Vetlesen, 2009), bringing us face-to-face with the need to recognize aspects of existence over which we have no control. Thus, anxiety forces us to confront ourselves. In this sense, anxiety is a responsibility toward ourselves and a necessity to challenge and over-come the difficulties of life, to be able to see options and act upon them (Vetlesen, 2009).

Case illustration

Consider the case of Sara and Simon. (All cases in this book are real. Details that could identify the individuals described have been altered).

Sara, 58, married to Simon, 68, is the mother of three children and grandmother of two. She works as a teacher's assistant in a kindergarten for children with special needs. She derives much satisfaction from her work. Her relationship with her partner was always conflictual but she paid little attention to this. She was giving to those around her without limits and without expecting rewards. Three months before she arrived for treatment Sara was in a serious accident because of which her over-all physical and psychological condition deteriorated. Her injured foot was in constant pain, and her movement was limited. From an active and energetic woman, she became slow and experienced herself as heavy. She described experiencing deep distress and emotional turmoil, feeling constantly depressed, and having a hard time sleeping. The psychiatrist diagnosed her as having anxiety attacks and PTSD and prescribed anti-depressants and anti-anxiety pills.

The most painful experience she reported was the humiliating and insulting attitude of her husband. She described a disrespectful relation-ship, often verbally and emotionally abusive, expressed as silence and disregard. Sara was referred to the mental health clinic. During treat-ment, it became clear that the disregard experienced by her was gener-alized and expressed not only by her partner but also by her children and colleagues. Sara was overwhelming herself by filling up her day to the maximum. She would get up early and go to work, return home for a short break, and proceed to her daughter's home to help with the grandchildren. She was available to help all three children at any time, support her husband when needed, and care for her aging par-ents, cleaning and cooking in her remaining time. Recently her husband refused to sign for her credit line at the bank. She felt this as an insult and a sign of lack of consideration for her minimal needs. After her recent accident, her husband made it clear that she couldn't expect him to help her in times of need: "Don't expect me to hand you the night can." Her tendency to relieve those around her from any responsibility toward her and her willingness to live in the shadow of humiliation and disregard were the constant themes of her life. But it was her husband's refusal to help her when she was injured that confronted her with the lie she had been living, and destroyed her ability to go on pretending that all was well.

Sara's physical and emotional injury ruined the taken-for-grantedness in her experience. The permeability of the boundaries between the ontic and the ontological became unbearable and led to increased anxiety. This also served as a catalyst to asking questions about her being in the world, and became an epiphanic event, followed by a severe existential crisis. Such crises often erupt after a symbolically significant event in the person's life: traumas, losses, accidents, marriage, separation, the death of a loved one, a life-threatening experience, a new partner, drug use, adult children leaving home, reaching a personally significant age (turning 16, turning 40), and many more. Events like these may evoke intense reflection and questioning about personal suffering, mortality, a sense of justice or injustice, and personal limits. Each individual creates symbolic representations of existence that break down in existential crises. Such crises refer mostly to the moment when a person metaphorically hits the wall or reaches the bottom. During a full-blown existential crisis, everything may be too much and seem meaningless. The accident brought to the surface the sense of thrownness. Sara was forced to confront the symbolic foundations of her adult life: family relations, self-sacrifice, loyalty, and patriarchal values. It dramatized to her that the value placed on unconditional giving did not lead to mutuality. The existential threat came from the collapse of the existing order, and chaos overcame her experience. Her loss of control was mostly an expression of her inability to continue ascribing meaning to the values underlying her beliefs about family, which until this turning point she considered essential to her being. Her self-orientation lost directionality, and the future lost its meaning in the context of her lifelong project. Her behavior was unvarying, yet her experience became alien and void.

The term "existential crisis" relates specifically to the individual's realization that what used to be cannot continue, and that one is forced to choose. Not choosing is choosing to continue avoiding, bringing the inner and outer selves into conflict. Following the accident, Sara realized that her distress was inevitable. Schneider (2007) maintained that anxiety consistently emerges from the tension and relationship between limits and possibilities arising from freedom. It is what Jaspers called "limit situations" (Miron, 2012), in which human beings are said to have divergent experiences from those arising from ordinary events and situations. Under such conditions, struggle and suffering become inevitable. Yet such situations cannot be avoided or disregarded. The ensuing recognition must be that nothing in this world is stable, safe, and absolute; that there is no unconditional support. In "limit situations," there is first, awareness of the boundaries of consciousness, and second, a limit to personal ability that leaves us powerless and trapped. The human tendency is to avoid such situations, deny them, or ignore them. For Sara, the accident was a limit situation that confronted her with the recognition that her existence is associated with suffering and emotional harm, exploitation, and abuse. For years she accepted the situation and took it for granted. The accident forced her to step aside from this familiar path and recognize the possibilities arising from her anxiety.

Ultimate concerns

Yalom (1980) conceptualized four ultimate concerns in the human condition: death, freedom, existential isolation and meaninglessness, and the anxiety arising from being in the world.

Death

Yalom (1980, 2008) placed death and dying at the center of the ultimate concerns. Humans are aware that death is inescapable, ontological, and goes beyond a biological dictum. It is real, a clear fact of life. We cannot envision it as something abstract and generalized, but rather as our private death, to be expected as a finite reality. Most of the difficulty arises from its inevitability and the knowledge that there is no escape from it. Thus, an inner conflict arises from the contrast between the inevitability of death and our wish to be. How to be in a world belonging to death? Death consciously subverts our sense of belonging to the club of the living. It terrorizes us more than anything else. Fear of death exists at every level of human awareness, in the internal experience of existence, from the most conscious and intellectualized, to the darkest depths of the unconscious. Our finiteness is cruel, unjust, and unethical toward ourselves. Humans go out of their way to deny death or to escape from its tyranny. The inevitability of death is in sharp contrast with being alive and with the freedom of the individual. This connects to Anton Chekhov's (1921) reflection: "Death is terrible, but still more terrible is the feeling that you might live forever and never die." Yet by choosing the meaning of our own death while alive, we may score a victory over it. By doing so, everyday experiences successfully suppress and marginalize the presence of death in life.

The accident was the life event that undermined the taken-for-grantedness of Sara's life. She repeatedly described and analyzed her accident and the possibility of dying as a result of it. The anxiety of death first crept into her consciousness when she expressed unwillingness to remain in a rehabilitation unit adjacent to the geriatric department. Sara saw in this proximity a hidden message that the geriatric unit was the next and final stage. She felt the threat of becoming old, helpless, and dependent, with death occasionally peeking in, from behind. Her fear of becoming dependent was exacerbated by her husband's statement that he had no intention of supporting her as she aged and was likely to need it. The sharp passage from an experience of autonomy and physical and emotional competence to that of a limited person in need of assistance in intimate activities, such as washing up and going to the toilet, symbolized deterioration, and subsequent death. Her sense of control lost, Sara realized that she was no longer the same woman she used to be, that old age was knocking at the door, with loneliness, dependence, and helplessness in tow. The absurdity and meaninglessness suddenly became apparent, symbolizing death and finality.

Existential freedom

Individuals do not come into the world with a structured coherent map for living, yet they are responsible for their own being-in-the-world, their life plans, choices, decisions, and their subsequent outcomes. Sartre (1946/1965) said that "we are condemned to freedom." We are the sole authors of our world, life design, actions, and choices. This should give us a sense of the significance of assuming responsibility.

Being responsible for creating one's own world rests on interpretive rather than material grounds, and therefore, it is experienced as nothingness. The term "groundlessness" is used to describe the subjective experience felt when individuals confront existential freedom and the anxiety that may evolve when one encounters the reality of absolute self-responsibility. "To be aware of responsibility is to be able to create one's self, destiny, life predicament, feelings, and if such is the case, one's suffering" (Yalom, 1980, p. 218). Thus, the second inner conflict surrounding existence results from contrasting our consciousness of the experience of freedom, and the lack of objective grounds or measures, mixed with a deep need for structure and grounding.

This conflict is evident in Sara's dilemma regarding the possibility of divorce, stemming from the contradiction between her awareness of this possibility and the anxiety about its actualization. She is frightened by the possibility of freedom as well as by the potential loss of a "husband" who could care for her in an alien world of strangers. Despite evidence to the contrary, Sara also maintains that the option of divorce is not feasible for economic reasons. Her anxiety about freedom becomes evident when she examines the option of not being married and ceasing to be a "model housewife." Sara asks nothing for herself. She does not feel the freedom of entitlement to responsiveness to her needs or perceptiveness to her validated version of reality. She is frightened of becoming acquainted with the multiple options available to her. She does not think she is entitled to be angry and considers anger to be an entrapping emotion. She is constantly sacrificing and cannot recognize rights along with the responsibilities she carries toward her family. She maintains that voicing multiple complaints creates family tensions that can tip the balance and ruin everything. The increased pressure and anxiety cripple her ability to act. "Bad faith," which in existentialism is a denial of one's freedom, becomes an instrument that separates her options for freedom from the possibility of actualizing them.

Existential isolation

The meaning of existential isolation goes beyond loneliness. It involves the knowledge of being separated, alienated from your choices and from other beings. More fundamentally, it is the recognition of the unbridgeable gap between oneself and the world. Isolation is not relationship-dependent, and it may exist alongside satisfying relationships with others. The conflict precipitated by isolation is between our awareness of basic isolation together with our need to be protected and relational.

Existential isolation is concealed within the lived experience, in everyday and routine activities. Yalom (1980) pointed to the dilemma he called *fusion-isolation* as a key existential developmental task and believed that behind insecure attachment lies the fear of isolation. Existing is in the eyes of others. To feel alive, one continually needs affirmation and acknowledgment from the other (Sartre, 1943/1966). One of the key components of enduring unsatisfactory relationships is the terror of being alone, which is considered more unbearable than the relationship itself. One is likely to sacrifice oneself to the illusion of belonging.

Sara states that she wants nothing but quiet. She does all the chores at home, for her partner and for her children. She states that she never demanded anything and sacrificed herself for peace and quiet at home. Her loneliness is manifest in her difficulty to make decisions. Yet anxiety raises heavy doubts about the correctness of her decisions. Consequently, she feels trapped in loneliness, which further incapacitates her. She states that she will not leave her husband because of economic reasons, but what she appears to fear is loneliness. She describes the pain associated with verbal abuse, humiliation, and the petrifying silence of her partner in the face of her need to preserve the home and care for the children.

Existential loneliness is also manifest in the context of gender. Sara describes growing up in a patriarchal environment that marginalizes women. The dominant value women live by is the expectation to sacrifice themselves for the family and their men. Such sacrifice is a measure of the individual and social self. The sense of loneliness and isolation is dramatically illustrated in Sara's view of the future. As she described it earlier, following the accident, her husband's implicit attitude and explicit statement raised before her the terror of aging alone, without help and support. Paradoxically, the more she becomes aware of her isolation and loneliness, the more she takes on responsibilities at home and becomes increasingly dependent on bearing the load expected by her cultural environment. This makes her situation ever more threatening, as the danger of losing the sense of familiarity (reflected in Heidegger's concept of the uncanny or "unheimlich") becomes imminent—yet another illustration of the ontological suffocating the ontic.

The circle of loneliness, the isolation and estrangement arising from unfamiliarity escalates over time and becomes unbearable. The only way to overcome the resulting anxiety is to reaffirm and hang on to the taken-for-granted, the known, and the familiar, together with the suffering associated with such a position. By doing so, the bad faith is reaffirmed, and freedom curtailed.

Existential meaninglessness

Questions about the meaning of life haunt people in different phases and life situations. Why do we live? What do we live for? What do we live by? What is the meaning of life? Yalom's (1980) fourth ultimate concern is that human beings need meaning as a framework for interpreting the past, the present, and the future, and to construct a sense of control in overcoming nothingness and groundlessness. Thus, meaning becomes an issue of life and death. Life without meaning, as expressed in values and ideals that serve as critical frames of reference, may lead to despair and to alienation from self and the world. Suicide and various forms of self-inflicted harm are plausible solutions in such situations. The conflict associated with this fourth ultimate concern stems from the contrast between the expectations of meaning in an inherently meaningless world. It is difficult to tolerate the idea that beyond what we construct there is no meaning in the world. This experience of meaninglessness encompasses the unfairness of the world. To live the life of the absurd means rejecting a life that pursues specific meanings for our existence, as there is nothing there to be pursued.

The most dramatic experience of self-destruction, attempted suicide, is the result of a sense of helplessness and hopelessness, a feeling that there is no proper exit, and hostility toward the self and others, all of which point toward meaninglessness (Orbach, 2007). The individual concludes that life has no intrinsic value and significance and cannot find a reason to be. Self-injury or substance abuse act as temporal avoidance strategies, or what Frankl (1969/1988) referred to as "existential vacuum," and as a cry for meaning and authenticity. But there are situations in which the act of suicide may be associated with serious mental health challenges. Some argue that at that particular phase of the struggle, most individuals do not choose but rather commit suicide because of an acute mental condition. The counter-argument is that suicide does not reflect human determinism because not all people with the same mental condition commit suicide.

The lurking threat is the absurd

According to Kierkegaard, absurdity is limited to actions and choices of human beings arising from human freedom. Camus held that the world and human beings are not inherently absurd but rather reflect the voice of the screaming men and the irrational silence of the world inhabited by them (Golomb, 1995), as Munch's famous and disquieting painting shows. The realization that the absurd always prevails over the rational is experienced as frightening; therefore we make repeated attempts to escape it. The best-known path for escaping it is "bad faith" or "*mauviase foi*," in Sartre's words. Sara refuses to assume the responsibility arising from viewing herself as meaning maker. She separates the world from the meaning she attributes to it, concluding that her constructions (decisions, choices) exist out there separate from her. She becomes both the creator and the victim of this self-deception: "I'm cheating and allow myself to state that I'm not aware of it." To escape responsibility, we attempt to find accounts, justifications, and excuses that prove that we are not free in our meaning making but depend on external circumstances or subconscious forces stronger than we are. Sara's meaninglessness can be understood in the context of her interpersonal relations but also as an aspect of her social being in a patriarchal world leading to her alienation from herself.

To conclude, anxiety should be assumed as ontological, and as such, it is a distinctive disclosure of the world. In professional encounters, it is essential to shed light on the circle of anxiety and its outcomes. Most people try to objectify anxiety and bring it into focus to make it bearable or to deny it altogether. As social workers, we must understand the meaning of the crisis arising from such anxiety. What is the great threat in the life situation in which anxiety manifests itself? What are loss and betrayal at the level of individual experience? What are the consequences for the clients' sense of being in the world? What is it that breaks down and leads to a turning point after which the world can never be the same? These questions lead to an inevitable sense of the absurd. How do we experience this absurdity and what strategies can we deploy to avoid it? Hand-in-hand with the suffering, what possibilities are opening up as a result of the crisis? In other words, what are the challenges facing the individual experiencing both the absurd and freedom of choice? Can they coexist, and if yes, what kind of additional anxiety does such coexistence produce, and how does it affect the individual's being in the world? All these questions are in a dialectic relationship between the ontic and the ontological. They induce much pain and suffering arising from loss, but at the same time open up new possibilities. We look at some of these in the subsequent chapters.

2 Choosing, acting, and responsibility

The freedom of the individual reflects the encounter between the inner sense of being in the world and the external social and cultural context. Such freedom includes the expectation to take a position in situations subject to the limitations and pressures of real-life circumstances. Talking about self in existentialism van Deurzen-Smith (1997) wrote: "My self is not a thing, but a creation, which is momentary and fleeting unstable" (p. 49). Thus, one is participating in an ongoing construction of one's being in the world, including identity in action. This is in contrast to the observing self or the self-as-context theoretical orientation, according to which the self is above and beyond behaviors and choices. According to these perspectives the self is the result of pure awareness, a collection of images and words that does not get caught up in the content. This perspective frees the self of ideas and judgments that one imposes on oneself. According to the existential perspective, being oneself is to live up to one's facticity, freedom, and responsibility, to become aware that one has no unitary and solid self, but rather one exists through choices, projecting one's being-in-the-world. Thus, the self is not a reduction to an essence; there is no such thing as true self waiting to be exposed. By contrast, we rather speak about authenticity resulting from the struggle based on choices made by oneself. The self can be viewed as a process, continually created by one's choices resulting from engagement in one's situations. Perception of oneself as a stable and constant entity (e.g., self-esteem) may be in the service of one's bad faith, denying one's freedom. Accordingly, every choice and decision of any value to the Dasein faces the individual with the awareness of creating oneself.

Sartre's (1946/1948) statement that "existence precedes essence" sums up the main claim of existentialism. Our choices define our essence. He elaborated that "Man is nothing else but what he purposes, he exists only in so far as he realizes himself, he is therefore nothing else but the sum of his actions" (Sartre, 1948, p. 41) The outcome is that "At the heart of freedom is choice and at the heart of choice is action" (Cox, 2009, p. 5).

DOI: 10.4324/9781003322085-3

Therefore, there is no way to limit the consciousness of choice options or to design them according to given, preconceived patterns. First, the self exists as a given, and meeting the world, it defines itself ("being in the world"). Sartre rejects the deterministic view, arguing that human nature (or character) does not dictate our choices, but rather it is our various choices that determine and shape our personhood (van Deurzen-Smith, 1997). The following case illustration describes the complexities of being by choosing and acting.

Daniel, a 48-year-old man diagnosed with multiple sclerosis, sought the help of the social worker to address his fear of the future concerning his health. He felt that his life came to a halt and he could not accept it. He described himself as active before his illness, traveling abroad, reading, and meeting friends. Daniel confessed that since his illness he has locked himself up, has little or no patience, lacks motivation for any type of recreation, and is in no mood for social activities or for meeting friends. He described his agony at being impatient with his son, with whom he used to have close and warm relations, shared experiences, and common interests. In existential terms, the illness became his way of being in the world. He became the prisoner of the illness, and felt sorry for himself, helpless, miserable, dependent, and limited. He felt that he lost his freedom. He made attempts to free himself from the illness, from the unpredictability of his situation, and his inability to control it. His motto was that he must triumph over the illness, but he was not able to make the choices that would make this heroic view of himself in facing the disease come true.

Existential thought affirms the clear awareness of the inevitability of one's freedom in choosing from alternatives, together with the associated responsibility for one's choices (Krill, 1996). We are condemned to choose, and cannot choose not to choose (Sartre, 1946/1948). Individuals are always finding themselves in a life situation that is the embodiment of their being in the world. As Gabriel Marcel pointed out, individuals find themselves in situations they need to transcend by choosing and acting (Koenig, 1997). There is no escape from the world, its situations, and given circumstances, and there is no escape from the freedom to choose. The ontological freedom is total and does not fade away in given situations, such as illness, crisis, trauma, oppression, and other limiting forces. If personal freedom is considered situational, (at times free and at others not free), the meaning of ontological freedom loses validity. Such recognition is a source of anxiety, as humans are aware of responsibility as a source of power, as opposed to the tendency to run away from such awareness.

Daniel is thrown into a situation not of his making, but he is forced to choose and act. His attitude was that the illness denied his choices. He kept voicing his wish to be as he used to be before the illness. In the process, he acted in a manner that constructed for him a certain type of essence and personality. He could not see himself as part of such imposed passivity, and therefore he experienced the world as foreign to him. He felt he lost his freedom to external factors. Sartre (1943/1966) described two types of freedom: an ontological one, which is part of being human, and a situational one, arising from everyday existence. The act of choice takes place in concrete, given situations that limit the universe of possibilities for choosing and makes the choices final. People like to think of freedom of choice as what May (1983) called "freedom of doing." Yet we cannot avoid the questions of how much freedom is available for action and how many obstacles are in the way. Thus, in existential thinking, the focus is on the freedom of being, which is embodied in the attitudes adopted toward one's situation. Daniel tries to avoid the anxiety by adopting persuasive strategies to convince himself and others, including his social worker, that he is not free, therefore should not and cannot choose. Superficially, he is focused on what he can do to overcome the limitations imposed by the illness that makes him weak and helpless. Deep down, however, he fails to focus on his ontological freedom and sees himself as a chooser. This limits his alternatives, which nevertheless are always present. Yalom (1980) pointed out that people often have a wider range of choices than they perceive. Sartre (1943/1966) argued that human beings live in anguish, not only because life is miserable, but because we are "condemned to be free" and doomed to create ourselves, no matter how limited our options are. Since we have been thrown into the world (Heidegger, 1927/1996), our sense of groundlessness (the lack of a master plan and structure) feels innately threatening to our Dasein and denies us a stable foundation for choice making. Daniel was seeking such a master plan that could return to him what he had lost, trying to circumvent the experience of being doomed to recreate his being.

This lack of a predefined plan, together with an absurd existence that presents infinite choices to us is responsible for the "anguish of freedom" (Sartre, 1943/1966). Anxiety arises from the necessity to make choices and the power of our freedom to choose. The resulting dread can become paralyzing, as illustrated in the following example.

Tal, a woman in her 30s, is regarded by others as highly intelligent and talented in creative arts, music, and drawing. She is on welfare, having been diagnosed as mentally ill. She has been known to various mental health services ever since she was a youngster. She attempted suicide several times, and her arms are full of cuts, the scars of failed suicide attempts. She describes her life as full of sadness, alienation, and estrangement of the self, despair, and existential emptiness. This negative view of life is exacerbated by aggressiveness, acting out, hostility, and a general lack of interest in others. She worked with several social workers, but never found one who she thought met her needs. She said the professionals passed judgment on her and called her irresponsible. Tal concluded that the mental health system was rotten to the core, and the people working in it were arrogant and doing more harm than good to their clients. Instead of taking responsibility for problems inherent in the system, they pass on the problems to their clients and pressure them to make choices. She believes that the emptiness and inability to choose and decide are beyond her control, and that the world is cruel to her. From an existential standpoint, Tal refrains from creating meaning, and evades the freedom to move beyond facticity and become a person who is not defined by her current situation alone.

Yalom (1980) suggested that the freedom to choose comes with the will to be alive to self-creation, in control of one's destiny. Tal believes that "her destiny is to suffer and be wounded and vulnerable." She keeps citing her boredom with life as an ongoing, overarching theme. It includes everything except caring for her cat. She believes that her helplessness, emptiness, and inability to decide and act are beyond her control, beyond the options available for her to choose from. The belief that the world is cruel is used to avoid choices. From an existential viewpoint, the moment she accepts this predetermined course of fate, she renounces her ontological freedom. Existentially speaking, her perception of life events expresses the limitations imposed by the world and the lack of freedom, which together have entrapped her. Her experience of being under the control of ill-intentioned others, including professionals, saps her strength and competence. Consequently, she feels abandoned and lacks the ability to actualize her choices. She cannot contain the dialectical relationship between situational facticity and ontological freedom of choice, and navigate between the two. When she says: "I had no choice," she really means, "I chose this alternative rather than another that I was unwilling to choose."

Van Deurzen (2010) wrote: "We are our own future and we choose what we become in action, even though much of the time we do not accept this responsibility and pretend it is not so. Our actions speak louder than our words. We are what we do and what we do is what creates our self and our life for the future" (p. 84). Existentially, every act and every attitude must be considered a choice. The result is increased anxiety: "the overwhelming experience of freely choosing results simultaneously from the ever-present confrontation with a limited set of alternative possibilities, in combination with our all-too-human failure to ultimately justify which of the many possible actions we should perform" (Eshleman, 2011, p. 44). Thus, we cannot know the outcome of our choices, and cannot understand the world in which we make them beyond our limited capacity arising from illusions of certainty and necessity. Choices and decisions are usually made without guarantee of the validity of the values guiding them. We cannot fulfill "the wish to be protected, to merge and to be part of a larger whole" (May & Yalom, 2000, p. 285). The choices we are facing make us dizzy, and the absurd is always lying in ambush. Anguish in the Sartrian sense is the feeling of moral responsibility that accompanies the necessity to choose and the recognition that one can never obtain a final verdict about the correctness of one's choice or of any alternative choices. The paradox of freedom is resolved only by confronting the boundaries of the facticity of the situation (Moustakas, 1995). The next case illustrates the dialectic, conflict, and paradox described previously.

Nibal, a 45-year-old Muslim woman, has been married for 25 years and is the mother of four children, aged 12 to 24. She came to the welfare agency seeking means to stop the violence of her husband against her ("Help me please to know what I can do to make my husband stop beating me and screaming at me"). Nibal tended to deny the violent nature of her partner, and attributed his outbursts to life pressures, particularly economic, the involvement of others in their lives, or things she may have done to trigger the violence. Although she is not satisfied with her marriage, she stays in it because she does not believe in her ability to choose and make changes. She reiterated her belief that women's happiness can exist only within marriage. She tended to use Arab proverbs that stressed the importance of marriage despite the negative circumstances, for example, "the shadow of the man is preferable to the shadow of the wall." She refused to consider alternative scenarios, such as separation or calling the police, because such actions may have unpredictable personal, social, and cultural implications. From an existential standpoint, at times of crisis or pain, one confronts endless choices, including a total change of one's life. Violence and the sense of failure of her marriage confronted Nibal with the freedom inherent in the obligation to make choices. Anxiety enhanced the recognition of being thrown into the world with no guarantees. She experienced her life as trapped inside her family, in a cultural environment controlled by collectivistic values, crippling her ability to act. She seemed certain about the expected societal and family reaction toward her. In situations of this type, the option of bad faith, considering oneself completely subjected to facticity is a tempting one. Turning away from anguish, according to Sartre, does not mean overcoming it, but rather hiding from it in bad faith. Therefore, Nibal perpetuates her unbearable situation under the pretext that she has no resources to reorganize her life. In doing so, she is forced to sacrifice her freedom of choice in exchange for fictitious security. Nibal has a negative view of herself: "I kept looking in the mirror and telling myself: 'I'm glad my husband was willing to marry me; I'm not pretty and never stood a chance for a more successful marriage.

I've to come to terms with what I'm involved in and thank God for the opportunity to have a family.' "

Existential theory maintains that our self-defining choices are not random, impulsive, or capricious. They entail commitment to critical reflexivity on one's internal and external facts. This reflexivity is associated with a "fundamental project" ' (Sartre, 1943/1966) representing the totality of modes of being in the world, unifying a consistent set of choices and actions that a person commits himself to. The project of being is a fundamental choice because it regards one's self as a totality in a particular environment and circumstances. The situations described by Nibal, Daniel, and Tal are not crude, factual givens; rather, they are constituted through the fundamental project that ascribes value to different ways of relating to the world. In each of the previous cases, the situation they face is not of their own creation, but they are responsible to assign meaning to it through their freedom to choose and to overcome bad faith. For Nibal, the key issue is to come to terms with the question of what the basic project of her life might be. Over the years, she considered family and parenting as her life project. She told her social worker that she often sits on the porch at night and asks herself whether marriage and family are the only things that give meaning to her life, and if so "why does she feel so bad about herself?" She asks: "Where do I get all this dissatisfaction so deeply seated within my soul?"

To experience one's freedom, it is necessary to know the limitations that structure one's given reality. This is a condition for choosing and for transcending anxiety and fear. Yalom (1980) maintained that decisions and choices produce anxiety because their realization negates other options that cannot be realized (Robert Frost's "road not taken"). One needs to renounce possibilities that may never be offered again. Such situations therefore generate pain. Additional anxiety arises from the recognition that choices made in the past affect the present and the future. Nibal's experience is one of entrapment created by her own past choices that affect her present and future. She chose a partner and married. Subsequently, she chose to stay in the marriage despite her suffering. In doing so she dug an existential tunnel along the path she chose. Any present choice is perceived as worse than the previous one because it has implications for her children and family. Such a closed-circuit trajectory creates a sense of a process of escalation leading to the belief that one's past decisions determine the future.

The three cases discussed reflect what Jaspers described as a "limit situation" (Koenig, 1997), when questions about the freedom of choice collide with bad faith. The understanding that it could have been different exposes us to the knowledge that we are subject to freedom and choice. The choice is not of an either/or type; rather, it reflects the depth of existence. As Yalom (1980) pointed out, every confrontation with an existential given involves a choice either to avoid dread or to move forward despite it.

The need to choose and act produces existential guilt. The guilt involves a feeling of unrest that evolves in our consciousness that we are untrue to ourselves and missing out on something. Such anxiety does not arise because of not meeting others' expectations or misbehaving, but rather because of the recognition that the choices we make are harmful, alienating, hostile to the realization of our being in the world. The conflict is the result of the tension between what we are and what we wished to be our ideal. At the heart of such guilt is a sense of self-betrayal resulting from the failure to follow the moral mission of our personal life. Some of the key expressions of such experiences are a deep sense of letdown of oneself, low and negative self-value, a sense of failure, and even self-hate. The outcome of our freedom is that we experience ourselves as forever recreating ourselves as judging and condemning our own life. This is why Nibal, together with the inner voice of bad faith, heard another voice saying "I'm not alive. . . . This is not what I wanted from life. What am I alive for?" These voices represent Nibal's struggle to accept herself as subjective and able to transcend facticity, not to be at the mercy of outside forces. In doing so, she faces the dilemma of responsibility.

Responsibility

One's primary responsibility is to accept one's mere being, and the absurdity involved in it. Camus (1942/1955) maintained that suicide was the rejection of freedom and flight from the absurdity of reality. In the ever-presence of the possibility of suicide, instead of fleeing from the absurd meaninglessness of life, he advised embracing life passionately and focusing on the question of what makes life worth living. This decision guides choices and actions in every situation. Complementing such a position is the assumption of full responsibility for the choices and the subsequent actions taken. We follow Sartre in emphasizing that if we are ontologically free, we are always free and cannot surrender our freedom without empowering the forces aiming to victimize us. Existential freedom should not be confused with freedom from responsibility (May, 1979; Thompson, 1992); yet, there is no escape from freedom, as there is no escape from responsibility. Cox (2009) wrote:

> For existentialist philosophers, freedom is not essentially about what people are at liberty to do, about what they are able to do or allowed to do and so on, but about each person's responsibility for whatever they do or do not do in every circumstance in which they find

themselves. . . . Freedom is not freedom from responsibility, freedom is having to make choices and therefore having to take responsibility.

(p. 45)

Since we are the sole creators and choosers of our attitude toward our life, we are responsible for facts such as our genes, the place where we were born, and past family history. To be responsible, we must construct an ongoing process of reflection about our relationship with other people and the world. Since nothing outside forces us to act in any particular way, we are completely responsible for the outcomes of our actions and the resulting anguish. No one can assume responsibility for these choices and the subsequent anguish but ourselves. Along these lines Nibal, Tal, and Daniel are fully responsible for their choices and ensuing consequences, even in the case of a severe illness, such as multiple sclerosis and mental illness, or intimate partner violence. Social workers are expected to reaffirm their clients' identity as choosers, with the associated anxiety and responsibility.

Yalom (1980) maintained that every important choice involves action. A choice is not valid without a preferred mode of action. Promoted by existential thinking, such radical freedom has both positive and negative consequences. The positive dimension has to do with the fact that people determine how they live. The negative one reflects the dictum that people are condemned to make decisions and to accept their implications, together with the responsibility, without explanations or excuses. The enormous burden of responsibility of free human beings results from the constant anguish associated with such responsibility.

Every choice reflects one's being in the world. Additionally, we must face the dilemma between responsibility toward oneself and responsibility toward the other (more about it in the chapter Being with and among Others). Our responsibility toward ourselves as a loyal and authentic subject transcends our freedom. Responsibility toward the other is conditional to transcending one's freedom. Based on our dialectic perception, which combines the individual with the social, we suggest that Daniel needs to be responsible for finding authentic choices for actions, actualizing his freedom in his relationships with his son concerning parental values. Tal constructed her being as devoid of relationships with other people, alienating herself from others. From Levinas's perspective, there is no meaning to individual existence without accepting the burden of responsibility toward the other (Levinas, 1947/1987). Tal needs to develop her ability to transcend her choices in critical situations. This way, she constructs her being toward the other. Nibal must transcend her freedom of choice mostly toward her children, while considering the social and cultural environment in which she lives.

In sum, social workers are expected to understand individuals' being in the world and the way they experience the anxiety arising from the burden of choice, action, and responsibility. The professional should ask: What is the attitude chosen by my clients regarding their freedom to weigh the consequences and the circumstances of their actions? The ways in which individuals choose their actions vis-à-vis the consequences of these actions are based on the courage to choose the future.

3   The meaning of meaning

The search for meaning is one of the dominant forces in the existential experience of individuals. The meaning comes in response to the question, why? The responses reflect the purpose and value of one's being. Meaning is simultaneously abstract and concrete, most limited and broadest. Meaning is a long-term concept unifying the life span, simultaneously reflecting the immediate action and moment. On the one hand, it is personal, as every individual has a private understanding of meaning. On the other, meaning makes sense not only to individuals but also to couples, families, communities, nations, and humans at large. Such multidimensionality, together with its nuances, makes the experiential dimension of this concept larger than life, difficult to grasp, pretentious, and slippery. At the same time, it is experienced as a practically present and immediate preoccupation, and as a steppingstone in giving value to life.

Experience and meaning are inseparable because they co-create each other, and as such, both are part of the process and its outcome. This duality is reflected in various synonyms we use in language for meaning, such as purpose, cause, aim, interpretation, intent, value, and worthwhileness—all representing both the end of the journey and the road to get there.

Joseph, 70 years old, went to see his family doctor. His joints hurt and his walking became insecure from one day to the next. The doctor listened to him and gave his condition a name, "arthritis," and told him that it is common at his age, and that he can expect it to get worse. Another prescription and another bottle in his medicine cabinet. On his way home from the clinic, he stopped at a small neighborhood café and started thinking: They all say I'm old because they judge me by my ID card. I don't feel old. Young people's legs hurt too. I survived death several times and didn't let it come close to me. To say that I don't think about it often would be a lie. I'm trying to share my wisdom with youngsters, but they often look at me as an old person and disregard what I have to say. Nevertheless, I regard myself as a wise man. I made many mistakes in my life, but I can talk about them and learn from them. I often forget things that happened recently, but remember

DOI: 10.4324/9781003322085-4

how she looked 35 years ago. These thoughts illustrate social definitions, personal experiences and the need to construct meaning that combines all the contradictions and complexities. Without active meaning
making, the individual remains passive, exposed, and in great pain and
turmoil. Meaning serves as a shell, protecting against nothingness yet
allowing experiencing everything. As noted previously, meaning making for Joseph is a compass that helps him know where he is headed,
why things are as they are (his age, his illness), and what accounts for
the way things are. Thus, meaning is a road sign for the end of the journey and for the path to get there. He can now choose to frame his health
situation as a source of suffering and predict a bleak future or regard it
as a challenge and fight back, use it as a stepping stone to place himself,
as a choosing self, in the foreground, and the illness and old age in the
background.

There are several issues surrounding the definitions of meaning (Hill,
2018; Landau, 2017; Leontiev, 2013; Spinelli, 2007). An attempt will be
made to conceptualize and illustrate these by using an example of wom-
en's attempt to redefine meaning in a hostel for surviving prostitution.

1) Meaning is a mental construct, part of a mental web created by
   active framing that combines experiences with their interpretation.
   The structure of meaning underlies the goal and aim of the experience, shaping the ways of being in the world. Meaning is created and
   expressed as a continuum, with its strength ranging between two
   extremes of absolute meaning and absolute meaninglessness. Meaning is related to growth and wellbeing as opposed to distress and
   its expressions, such as depression, addiction, and so on. Hanah,
   36 years old, has been working in prostitution since she was 17. She
   spent most of her life thinking of herself as bad, flawed, the black
   sheep and disgrace of her family and peers. She started a career in
   prostitution through a man who turned out to be a pimp, but who
   appeared to her at the time to love, care for, and protect her. People
   in her environment saw the relationship as exploitive and considered
   the man to be a pimp who takes advantage of her, but she refused
   to accept this meaning and continued even when he forced her into
   sexual relations with strangers. At the time, the meaning she ascribed
   to this was that when she loves she will do anything for her lover. . . .
   Her inner sense of alienation from the normative world was enhanced
   by the encounters with social control agents such as police, social
   workers, and jail staff. Over the years, the suffering, the violence, and
   the betrayals emptied her out and she was increasingly experiencing meaninglessness with respect to who she was, what her life was
   about, and what her prospects were. She entered the hostel stating
   that she wanted to break with prostitution and create new meaning
   in her life.

2) Meaning has an inherent structure; in other words, it delineates boundaries of possibilities. It legitimizes certain experiences and discards others. Meaning has an outward dimension but can be explored and understood through introspection rather than from the outside. Joint meaning makes it possible to transcend experience and specific situations, signaling that the whole is more than the sum of its parts. Individual meaning creates a hierarchical structure with differential value, importance, and significance attributed to experiences concerning being in the world. Individuals differ from each other regarding the specific types, numbers, and depths of the sources of meaning, as well as the combination of what is constructed as meaningful. For example, people differ in values related to their family history and relationships, ideals, traditions and culture, legacy, religion, and life activities. Similarly, they differ in their attitudes toward the hardships of life, awareness of sociopolitical issues, and activism. The construction of new meaning for Hanah was facilitated by the process of moving from delegitimized to legitimized life by attempting to create a new narrative of herself. The need to make a living, to gain acceptance, and to seek warmth and care are all reframed in light of this changed narrative. Moreover, being reflective and introspective made possible the acquisition of the strength needed to resist old temptations and to commit to the new meanings arising from changed priorities. This in turn was helpful in examining and accepting the gap between her social identity and the changed personal identity, and assigning new meaning to the gaps between the two. In her interactions with the social worker, Hanah's critical task became to master skills and knowledge related to how she can bridge between normative meanings and those she was familiar with from her past life, and be prepared to pay the price for it. A good example is the effort she made to break away from her pimp's temptations and threats, and change her plan for economic survival based on her new priorities.

3) Dialectically, meaning creates coherence over time and provides continuity, order, and confirmation that go beyond a set of specific goals. But meaning is also temporary, it is challenged by events, and changes over time (age is a case in point). As a result of such changes in one's meanings, conflicts and inconsistencies with the previous meaning systems are inherent in being, making it possible to adapt to life situations. This existential process was present in Hanah's attempt to reconstruct meaning from humiliating and degrading experiences, and from obstacles that strengthened her in her quest for both behavioral and spiritual change.

4) Meaning is always relational and intentional in the sense that there are always objects to which meaning is directed. Thus, meaning is always located within intersubjective relationships within a social

and cultural context. In the process of meaning reconstruction, Hanah needed to reorient her intersubjective relational activities from the pseudo-love and warmth inherent in prostitution to those who reinforce and support her new version of herself and her future life. For example, she needed to mobilize the strength to accept the fact that there can be a substitute for selling her body in changed relational structures that oppose exploitation by others or of others.

5)   Meaning is expressed within a linguistic structure created in the dialectic process between the experience and language. The language is both subjective and socially constructed. The construction process occurs through the creation of narratives organized in a hierarchical structure by subjective judgment about their importance. Therefore, meanings co-construct "fundamental projects" with master narratives, which become the mirror of one's being in the world. The narratives open the possibility for construction of a clear subjective perspective of life. At the same time, the narratives, by their mere existence, reflect the tension between themselves and related life events. Hanah's fundamental project at this time was to work with women persuading them to leave prostitution. To accomplish this, she used the narrative of her life story, emphasizing the language leveled against her by use of the word "whore" to define her being. She gradually identified the gap between this word and between "sex-work for money." This linguistic gap became a critical symbol of the turning point in her view of herself.

6)   Meaning is a complex dynamic structure, ever-emerging, multidimensional, and not necessarily coherent. There are fluctuations of meanings and values throughout life. Finally, we must distinguish between global and situational meaning. Global meaning refers to the inner structure of values and beliefs concerning the self and others; situational meaning refers to occurrences in one's life. We should not assume harmonious relationships between the two, as global and situational meanings often are in conflict, resulting in pressure to reconcile them. For example, in cases of intimate partner violence, male batterers encountered by the authors in the course of their work adopted a global moral attitude of opposing intimate violence, while at the same time, in many life situations, they provided moral accounts and justifications of their violent behavior. The complexity in Hanah's reconstruction of meaning arises from the constant dynamics of figure and ground between her new and old meaning. At her new normative workplace, it became known that she used to be a prostitute. Suddenly her normative identity was threatened as her old one moved from ground to figure. The challenge became to avoid rejection by reinforcing the place of the global meaning at the forefront.

Meaning in existential thought

Two perspectives have been identified in existential thinking concerning meaning (Wong, 2012). One emphasizes the "dark side" of the human condition, the inherent meaninglessness leading to anxiety, suffering, absurdity, and death. This is evident in the recognition of ontological insecurity, particularly in situations of crisis, suffering, and pain. In these situations, the individual must face the shaky basis and doubtful conditions of one's very existence. Yalom (1980) pointed out that individual meaninglessness evolved from the perception of an inherently meaningless world. This belief results from experiencing the inability to cope with the anxiety evoked by basic life givens, such as mortality and aloneness. The challenge then is to find meaning in an apparently meaningless world. Meaningfulness makes it possible to cope with anxiety while realizing its continuous existence (Spinelli, 1989)

The other perspective is rooted in what Frankl (1969/1988) called "the will to meaning" as an innate human drive to find direction, value, and coherence in personal existence. This implies having depth and a positive attitude to life, beyond merely surviving. Such a perspective "capitalizes on the uniquely human capacity to discover and create meanings and values out of the raw and often painful experiences" (Wong, 2010, p. 85). At the heart of this perspective is the belief that people have freedom and desire to view their life as meaningful, and they are motivated to reinstate meaning in response to life challenges and threats, based on their strengths and competencies (Batthyany & Russo-Netzer, 2014). Unlike from the previous perspective, here meaning is perceived as originating in inner strength, and not in facing the anxiety resulting from lack of meaning. In this perspective, meaninglessness is the failure to find sufficient answers to ultimate existential concerns, not a built-in feature of existence. Frankl (1969/1988) referred to a state of meaninglessness as "existential vacuum," a phenomenon characterized by a subjective state of inner chaos, self-alienation, boredom, numbness, apathy, void, and emptiness. It is a state in which one loses one's inner sense of direction. The feeling is that there is a lack of autonomy, nothing to value, nothing to live for, nothing to struggle for, and nothing to hope for. From this perspective, the state of meaninglessness is the result of failing to capitalize on the will to meaning, and not of nothingness.

In this book, we adopt a dialectic logic that recognizes the opposites of two or more forces or themes which contradict and mutually negate each other, yet coexist and are ontologically interdependent (Baxter, 2004). Human existence is located between the two dimensions noted previously: that of nothingness and ontological insecurity, and that of meaning creation and self-validation through the process of creation and subsequent choice from a variety of possibilities. In Spinelli's view (2007) existential positions must avoid imposing separation between mean-inglessness and meaningfulness, and ascribe similar weights to both in examining existence. DuBose (2016) wrote that "Meaninglessness, there-fore, is not the absence or privation of meaning but a *different kind* of meaning" (p. 286). The following example illustrates both perspectives described previously.

Case illustration

At the time of the intervention, Debora was an 82-year-old Holocaust survivor and a widow. She was referred to psychiatric daycare, following psychiatric hospitalization after trying to commit suicide by swallowing pills. She was diagnosed with major depression after her 42-year-old son died of cancer. He left behind a wife and six children. In the three months of hospitalization, Debora repeatedly said: "Many don't get to my age. I'm 82 and lived long enough. I want to die, to return home and take the pills. This time I'll succeed. Why live?" She describes growing up in East-ern Europe in a well-to-do ultra-Orthodox family, with a brother two years older than she. During the Holocaust, in 1943, the entire family was deported to a concentration camp. Her parents were killed, but she and her brother survived and emigrated to Israel. She married a Holo-caust survivor and had two children, a son and a daughter. She chose a traditional religious lifestyle, learned fashion design, and worked in a large factory where she was in charge of about 100 people. Her husband worked as a private entrepreneur and was quite successful. She describes a rewarding financial and professional life. She felt that she lived a mean-ingful life, particularly in view of the damages inflicted by the Holocaust on the entire family. Her husband died 11 years before the intervention. She accepted his death, stating that someone always goes first. She stayed busy with her design work from home, and had a rich social life. She found particular meaning in telling the story of her survival during the Holocaust to the younger generations and joined the groups participat-ing in the "March of the Living" in concentration camps. Her contribu-tion was recognized, and she was awarded various prizes. At the time of hospitalization, she perceived herself as being "in ruins." Her son's death devastated her emotional and mental world, and her view of jus-tice collapsed. She feels that if in the past she could continue and cope despite the losses, today she needs to cope with losses that seem beyond her comprehension and ability to give meaning. This time, the suffering seems unbearable to her. She's angry at God and has an account to settle with Him. She feels that she has paid enough over the course of her life and does not deserve this last blow.

Debora's story illustrates the dialectic described previously. The drive and desire for meaning, as the key factor in the first approach, can be identified at every step in her life. Assuming that we each possess a healthy core, according to Frankl (1946/1969), we must not ask what the meaning of our life is, but rather recognize that it is we who are being asked. Following the Holocaust, Debora's sense of being was strengthened by a surge in her freedom of will, the will to the meaning of life (Frankl, 1969/1988). Facing the questions arising from her losses helps her overcome the hardships and traumas of life, and the impending death and destruction. She develops the ability to choose how to respond to the unavoidable suffering and is able to ascribe meaning to her life despite the tragedy she lived through. Wong (2012) said that meaning is "highly idiosyncratic" because one's sense of meaning is based on personal history. Debora married, built a family, and started a new life. All these are actualizations and the translation into action of her values, and they give purpose to her life. Debora achieves self-transcendence in life, her continued belief and commitment to eternal values give her the strength to cope. Frankl believed that we cannot *make* meaning, but that we reveal meanings that make us truly ourselves, *find* them, and (*re*)*connect* with them. Debora feels that her life brings fulfillment because of (a) awareness that one's life is being directed and motivated by purposeful and valued life goals; (b) feeling that her existence is significant, important, and of value to others (the world); and (c) achieving a sense of coherence associated with inner logic and ensuing orientation (Hill, 2018).

The second perspective is related to the human realization of facing nothingness. The loss of her son at old age crippled Debora's habitual sense of meaning in life, structurally undermined her usual meaning system (e.g., being a good mother) destroyed her self-worth and integrity as a woman, together with her self-identity, values, and purpose in life. In her current situation she finds it beyond her ability to continue making meaning. Reflecting about meaning occurs usually at key junctures in life, before critical choices and life decisions in the face of upheavals in life and trauma. Trauma interrupts the coherence of life and raises the question of what life means when such dreadful things happen (Hill, 2018). Debora's initial meaning and sense making gave in to the darkness of meaninglessness and nothingness. She realizes that her previously successful paths to meaning making have failed, and as Sartre would say, she is condemned to be free to choose another set of meanings, which she fails to do. Sartre (1943/1966) maintained that humans have difficulty recognizing that meaning is not in the factual reality but in the attitude toward it. Denial of freedom to choose (bad faith) leads to desperation and suicide, or ideation about it. Debora experiences the randomness of existence and the lack of sense in factuality. She faces nothingness, existential angst, and loss of control. Her experience comes close to what Camus called the absurd resulting from the conflict between the human scream for meaning and the irrational silence of the world vis-à-vis the pain (Golomb, 1995). Such absurdity leads to an anxiety-ridden relationship between the individual and the world. Debora realizes that the power of meaning she achieved cannot cancel the absurdity of the "black hole" that is about to swallow everything. The result is estrangement, exile, and hopelessness. In the conflict between rationality and absurdity, the former has lost, and the outcome for Debora is depression and death, together with the destruction of her relating to God as a source of meaning. Debora denies herself freedom and responsibility to choose from the available possibilities as a result of the facticity of her son's death. She cannot see herself as being guided by meaning (e.g., building a family) as she did after the Holocaust. In this sense, she acts as if she has no freedom to choose.

Narrative

Narratives serve as a metaphor to understand how individuals construct, integrate, and order their perceptual experiences by choosing to omit or add details, and how they frame and reframe what is consistent with their sense of identity (Sarbin, 1986). Human beings resort to narratives to actively strive for meaning and sense in their life. Our interaction with the world is interpreted mainly in symbolic language systems in the form of stories (Bruner, 1990; Josselson & Hopkins, 2015). Stories make life meaningful (Lurie, 2006; Neimeyer, 2000). A narrative is always told from the point of view of a particular attitudinal and emotional framework and worldview.

The power of narrative lies in intentionally ordering events in time along a continuum and finding causal relations between them to develop ontological meaning and coherence (Goldie, 2014; Linde, 1993). Ricoeur (1984) wrote that in a narrative the past, present, and future are intertwined and mutually co-constructed. The narrative enables reflection on the past events and choices that led to the current situation, and opens future possibilities, constructing one's existence and self (Adams, 2018; McAdams, 1996; Goldie, 2014; Schechtman, 2011). Life is not a continuous and clear story, but a conjuncture of stories, at times constant, at others changing in time, places, and people. Stories often intertwine and occasionally contradict one another. A self-narrative "organizes the 'micro-narratives' of everyday life into a 'macro-narrative' that consolidates our self-understanding, establishes our characteristic range of emotions and goals, and guides our performance on the stage of the social world" (Neimeyer, 2004, pp. 53–54). The following case is an illustration of the construction of macro-narrative.

Halima, a 35-year-old Muslim woman, has been married for 17 years. She experienced violence throughout her entire life, including child abuse, and all forms of intimate partner violence, including sexual, physical, psychological, verbal, and economic, to the point of attempted murder. Her first micro-narrative was one of humiliation, helplessness, fear, and overall feeling doomed to suffer. Her second micro-narrative was one of obedience and patriarchal family structure, in which the woman is expected to keep the violence private, avoid involving control or helping agents, and act according to strict rules of problem solving within the extended family. At the same time, she gradually evolved an additional micro-narrative, which told her that this was not the way she wanted to live for the rest of her life. She further developed a micro-narrative of a strong woman who will not give up despite suffering and poverty, and will try coping. Finally, she developed a micro-narrative to seek help and turned to a social worker. Her secret dialogue with the social worker led to reflection on all these micro-narratives and to the development of a macro-narrative as to what kind of life she envisions for herself (being in the world). She defined this as a "life of my own," by herself, to herself. She decided to seek treatment in a shelter, despite the cultural labels, restrictions, blame, and the overall cost such an act would incur. At the shelter, she decided to divorce her husband, despite his threats that he would murder her if she dared do so. Her decision to divorce united her various micro-narratives into a macro-narrative that became a catalyst to move forward, hiding and with little outside support.

Narratives are especially important in experiences of distress and trauma because they help orient us in the world and cope with the angst that accompanies the ultimate concerns (Richert, 1999, 2002) in social and cultural contexts. Personal narratives are co-constructed in interaction with others, using language, which is inherently a social phenomenon (Richert, 2002). Our perspective is that social forces shape the dominant narratives that foster bad faith. Sartre said in *Nausea*: "This is what fools people: a man is always a teller of tales, he lives surrounded by his stories and the stories of others, he sees everything that happens to him through them; and he tries to live his own life as if telling a story. But you have to choose: live or tell" (Sartre, 1938/1969, p. 39).

Case illustration

Salem, a 51-year-old Muslim Arab man is married and has three children. For the past nine years, he has been living in a hostel for the mentally ill in the city, away from his native village. He works in a subsidized, sheltered factory. Salem describes his father as a dominant figure in his life, who made decisions for him and directed his life overall. He tried to please the father, without much success. After Salem graduated from high school, his father told him to pursue a legal-academic career, although he wanted to study journalism. He never graduated and started working in menial jobs in a factory. His father decided to get him married, chose a bride, and organized the wedding ceremony. Salem says that his relationship with his wife has been negative from the start. He began to suspect her of infidelity, and gradually became violent toward her. After a year and a half of violent marriage, he had a psychotic breakdown and was hospitalized. After he was released from the hospital, Salem returned home but did not take his medication, resumed the violent behavior, and was readmitted. Following his discharge from the second hospitalization, his wife refused to let him return home, and his father decided that he could not continue living in the village. His father decided that he should move to a hostel in another city, where he has been living for nine years. Salem feels ostracized and humiliated because of his wife's and his parents' refusal to let him return home. Even when he goes occasionally to the village, he seldom leaves the home of his parents out of shame and because of restrictions imposed on him by his family.

He describes his situation as follows: "Today I live with the (hostel) residents, their lives are mine; their problems are mine. Sometimes they are talking about good things, most often they are not. The pressures keep me from moving forward and returning to Salem as I knew him; Salem who is not sick and lives with other people, outside. I'm not part of the community today, but part of the hostel and belong to the residents of the hostel." Salem relates that in the city where the hostel is located, he is also stigmatized. He knows it:

> "From the looks of the people outside, the way they treat me, the way they make me feel . . . that I'm different from them and they want to avoid me. . . . They think that I'm different from them." He describes humiliating acts such as children from the neighborhood throwing stones at him and others who live in the hostel. "As long as the community treats me this way, the feeling that I'm sick and worthless stays with me. The question that preoccupies me is: 'Why did it happen to me?' I think if only people would treat me differently . . . I'm preoccupied only with the bad thoughts I think because of the illness, and it hinders my progress."

To understand Salem's narrative, it is important to reflect on his being in the world in a particular social and cultural context. Dominant discourses point to power relations expressed in norms, values, ideologies, and institutionalized ways of constructing meaninglessness. The dominant narratives ascribe specific meanings to lived experiences. Salem's question, "Who am I?" is focused on the narrative identity of a mentally ill person. His goals and specific aims are limited and dictated by the same discourse. He cannot develop a coherent inner logic of his experiences with himself and others. He is an outsider, different from other people, marginalized, stigmatized, demoralized, and excluded. He becomes insignificant to others, particularly to his nuclear and extended family. This impairs his ability to create meaning that projects him into the future. He feels terrorized by the tyranny of prejudice toward mentally ill persons, and is a victim of this. He experiences existential loneliness in a hostile world. His self-image is one of a lesser human being, with no agency to create meaning. As a consequence, he is forced to view himself as part of his newly acquired peer group, with a transformed social identity. Yet he is aware of the fact that this identity was forced upon him. He still misses recreating and sharing meaning with "normal" people. The paramount question for Salem becomes whether he can create meaning under conditions of loss of control over the social and cultural forces active in his environment. By his *laissez-faire* attitude, Salem rejects the freedom to choose to be brave in the face of cultural and social impositions. He chooses the road of bad faith in his life narrative instead of attempting to create meaning.

Authenticity

Meaning is based on two basic questions that need to be answered: "What does it mean to live one's own life?" (Pollard, 2005, p. 171); and "How shall I live?" Yalom (1980). From an existential perspective, these questions are rooted in being authentic. Heidegger (1927/1996) perceived "authenticity" to encompass the capacity of individuals to take ownership of their existence. As such, authenticity, as a metaphor for the experience of one's true inner being, is difficult to live by, yet fundamental to one's existence. Authenticity should be examined along two dimensions: first, in the experience of the authentic person, there is no gap between values, behavior, and emotions and their overt expression. In popular terms, one is not fake. This is manifested in relationships with others and validated by them. Second, authenticity represents one's inner subjective truth and cannot be transferred. One cannot judge the other as authentic or not because the experience belongs to the individual alone.

In Halima's case, her authenticity evolved from gaps between her true values, behaviors, and emotions, and those by which she had lived for years. The acute awareness of the consequences of being inauthentic came when witnessing her husband beating their daughter because, in his words, "he knew that Halima didn't hurt anymore." Her feelings and behaviors overlapped, together with the understanding that faking had its price. Her decision to seek help, go to the shelter, and divorce exacted a heavy toll on herself and her children. Yet she was willing to pay it against the advice of her extended family. Being authentic to her inner truth was more self-realizing than the faking she had been practicing in the past. The death threats related to her decision of being authentic created a severe ethical dilemma for the social worker, who realized that being authentic in this case was life-threatening.

Kierkegaard pointed out that authenticity reflects a subjective truth, it is not a matter of "what" (a specific content or domain in one's life) but rather one of attitude toward decisions to be made (Golomb, 1995). Thus, authenticity is not a theoretical concept but rather it reflects how one needs to live based on one's definition of the truth, how one needs to act upon that truth, and in doing so, reaffirm this truth on an ongoing basis. The quality of authenticity as an expression of truth does not correspond to the overlap between thinking and reality, but rather to the experience of what gives meaning to life, what justifies one's effort to be, and even one's willingness to die for. Thus, authenticity is a strong and courageous expression of self, more so than honesty. It expresses a more demanding attitude toward the self and does not rely on the external, on the audience. Dependence on the audience, on "them," distances individuals from their subjectivity and undermines their responsibility. Therefore, the emphasis is on what one chooses and subsequently how one implements the choice.

To be authentic, one needs to be open to anxiety. Authenticity is achieved when one is aware of the givens of life and accepts subsequent anxiety arising from the realization that there is no transcendental meaning beyond the freedom of the individual. Authenticity demands the experience of *Angst*. One must be responsible for choosing one's existence, given the facticity of a particular situation (family, culture, and so on). This embodiment of anxiety in "existential guilt" describes the potential for authenticity and complete responsibility for one's unique "being" (Heidegger, 1927/1996). Kierkegaard personified this sense of anxiety of the freedom to be in the image of a man standing on the edge of a cliff, feeling the "dizziness" of looking down into the "abyss," yet also envisioning the numerous possibilities available to him to actualize his being. In actualizing one's freedom of being, a person must have faith in this "leap." In doing, one can project the self into the future (Golomb, 1995).

Courage is a precondition for actualizing authenticity over time. Courage in the ontological sense is the courage to be, without attempting to escape anxiety. This is "the courage of despair, the courage to take his despair upon himself and to resist the radical threat of nonbeing by the courage to be as oneself, to transform" (Tillich, 1952/1966, p. 140). Heidegger took this one step further, stating that inauthenticity is a mode of being in which the individual disowns oneself as a separate being. Consequently, we sacrifice freedom and responsibility for the need to be open and engage with what is presented to our existence through experience. In inauthenticity, one is detached from one's experiences, acts, and eventually existential responsibility (Spinelli, 2007). Such existence is rooted in the past and based on traditional ways that were learned and became part and parcel of one's life. Sartre (1943/1966) saw inauthenticity as bad faith, the refusal to make choices and take responsibility to avoid anxiety over the consequences of our actions.

Being aware of the existential task of authenticity dialectically gives meaning to life and simultaneously increases anxiety. In existential thinking, the conflict between the will to be authentic and anxiety fills the pre-reflective space. This leads to escape from the ultimate concerns of being human and losing one's self in denial. Existentialists perceive inauthentic existence as a source of psycho-social problems. The inauthentic individual pays an emotional toll for trying to evade existential problems, often experiencing it as functional and adaptive. Severe inauthentic situations may lead to polarization between the real and the false self and subsequent identity problems (Laing, 1960).

They

From the existential perspective, being is always relational. Thus, authenticity must be examined in relation to others. For Heidegger, genuineness is a quality expressing uniqueness. Genuineness and uniqueness start once the individual faces up to and stops conforming to social dictums. By contrast, inauthenticity is immersion in the everyday, confronting ritualized knowledge (ready-to-hand) regarding being-in-the-world. Heidegger named such individuals as *das Man*, who does not give account to himself and lets his existence, "I let my existence be determined and defined by others, thereby changing its meaning from existence to essence. My ownness becomes otherness and I lose myself by my own actions" (Golomb, 1995, p. 94). Conforming to everyday roles, expectations, and beliefs of "they" enables the individual to feel that it is possible to cover up and/or to run away from one's existential anxiety, including the anxiety about freedom, and "disownment of the self." The likely result of such an attitude is self-alienation. This state escalates the ignorance concerning the potential freedom arising from possibilities and choices, which then help realize authenticity. It should be recalled that inauthenticity can be functional in the adaptation of the individual to society and culture. The price paid is an uncanny existence that generates much anxiety.

Vlad's is a case in point, illustrating how living for "them" empties life of meaning. Vlad, 37, was born in Russia to highly educated parents. Throughout his life, he attempted to live up to his parent's expectations but failed systematically. He had no interest in higher education and was an outstanding athlete, organized challenging guided field trips, and loved dangerous sports such as car racing. After finishing high school, he enlisted in the Russian army to challenge himself and see how he handled extreme physical situations. After his army service, he worked in rescue teams where he saved people's lives and was much appreciated by his peers, and felt invulnerable. At that time, he met his wife, love at first sight, who loved his adventurous personality. The couple had three children. At 30, he immigrated to Israel with his family, and his life turned sour. In Israel, there was little knowledge of his glorious past. He started working in a factory, bought a house and a car, and made new connections and friendships. Three years later, Vlad was involved in a serious car accident, after which he experienced severe headaches, temporary paralysis, and numbness in his legs. Specialists identified some neurological problems, but no treatment was provided. He changed jobs often, without being able to cope with tensions and pressures, and kept losing his job. He was recognized as an invalid and received an allowance, but his economic situation deteriorated and became increasingly oppressive. He seemed to have lost not only his body in the accident but himself as well. He felt that he had failed in his manhood and in his ability to support his family, became passive, helpless, dependent on his wife, and unable to function as a father. Overall, he was feeling "like a wreck," "defective" in the eyes of others. He attempted to commit suicide by jumping out of a window but was saved by his wife who pulled him back. He was subsequently diagnosed as suffering from major depressive disorder. In his previous life, Vlad continually maneuvered himself into situations in which his uniqueness (courage, physical strength, and endurance) was defined by others. He was constantly focusing on the extent of the others' approval. His life circumstances enabled him to live this dreamlike image. After the accident, his life situation changed radically and his dependence on others was reaffirmed day after day. When his physical strength was lost, his entire existence became meaningless. His definition as man, father, husband, and breadwinner was replaced by one of dependence and weakness. He had severe difficulties accepting his new self, and concluded that the only solution to his changed position was death. The professional contact sought to help him recognize his changed situation whereby the dictum of the "they" needed to be replaced by a newly emerging "I".

Existentialists tend to think that authenticity is a result of revolt, following one's decision to be something one is not. Humans are assumed to possess an inner truth, which can bring the individual to break free from norms. Authenticity, therefore, creates an obligation for individuals to set their goals and priorities in a way that is coherent with their choices and commitments. Putting into effect life priorities goes along with cleaning out accounts and justifications involving self-defeating bad faith.

Existential anguish resulting from striving toward authenticity is conducive to the experience of freedom and the recognition that one can move beyond any situation controlled by "them" and their impositions. Authenticity becomes owning one's possibilities for being. This is why Heidegger tied authentic being with existential guilt through the concept of "being-toward-death." Recognizing death is recognizing finality together with the responsibility for the future (Pollard, 2005). Authentic acceptance of being-toward-death liberates from the illusion of the tranquility of a *das Man* mode of existence and enables authentic choices, actualizing possibilities, and accepting responsibility toward self and others.

From Camus' perspective, achieving authenticity is based on a Sisyphean attitude that accepts the inherently absurd human fate (Golomb, 1995). Absurdity reveals the inauthentic being but also points to the authentic struggle against everything in the self and in the environment that tries to reduce one to non-being (e.g., suicide). In existential writing, "the search for authenticity is a personal wager in a world where other outcomes are no more probable. But if this unique gamble succeeds, our prize is optimal: authentic selfhood" (Golomb, 1995, p. 177).

Case illustration

We illustrate the issue of authenticity through two case examples. The first is that of Ortal, aged 24, not married, and living with her grandparents who brought her up. Her father suffers from post-war trauma. When she was 4, he was hospitalized in a psychiatric facility and never returned home, moving from one institution to another. Her mother remained alone with four children, in a difficult financial situation. She sent Ortal to live with her grandparents in a different city, keeping the other three siblings at home with her. Ortal describes herself as the black sheep of the family, the problem child who was sent away from home because of the difficulties she created in growing up. Her mother said that she had no strength to care for her while raising her other children. Ortal was labeled as a slow learner. She received no help in her studies, and the children laughed at her for being away from home. Over the years, Ortal tried to hide her life story and was ashamed to talk about her hospitalized father. She attempted to present a "normal" family image, a happy, warm, and supportive one, with both parents living together. She was always careful about how she dressed and looked. She was preoccupied with what others would say about her, how much to reveal and how much to hide about her social identity, all the way struggling with shame, which was the leitmotif of her life. Despite the crises and difficulties, she remained hopeful regarding change. With help and guidance from a social worker, she started working with retarded children. She loved caring for children and was good at it. She made progress and became increasingly professional and empathetic with the children. Eventually, she met a young man, and their relationship became serious. Intimate relationships were difficult for Ortal because of her limited capacity to decide how much to hide and how much to reveal about her present emotional state and past biography. She experienced pain as the dominant motif of her life. At times she was sharing this experience with her social worker: "Perhaps I don't need to be in couple relationships! Perhaps I should just be myself and continue helping others."

Jaspers pointed out that people in everyday life attempt to cope with metaphysical issues related to existence by minimization and avoidance (Miron, 2012). As noted earlier, only under conditions arising from limit situations can individuals recognize their circumstances as final or temporal. Only failure, crisis, and despair can become an existential force bringing about attempts to get beyond the everyday understanding and face the tension between what and how to choose to construct the difficulty of being. As Kierkegaard framed it, the difficulty is the road (Golomb, 1995).

Ortal's relationship with the young man is a limit situation that reflects the ways in which she avoided confronting the demands required by authentic choices. One of the main definers of lack of authenticity is the attempt to evade responsibility for present situations and past life events. To be authentic means to be able to make decisions and choices despite anxiety, and to see the anxiety as an opportunity to live in accordance with values considered to be rewarding. To consider the range of possibilities, the individual needs to recognize the freedom, choice, and responsibility to decide. Authentic individuals perceive the world as a narrative created by themselves and experience the capacity to alter it. Such a narrative has no fixed or established structure, the everyday knowing of it disappears, and everything is new and challenging. This is a defenseless world, and one should be willing to contain the resulting anxiety.

Ortal experiences her relationships with herself and the world, as well as her life history, as entrapment. Her inauthenticity results from the denial of the fundamental existential assumption that she is free and responsible for her life, which she experiences as bad faith. Life is perceived as unidimensional: anxiety, shame, and pain come together in internal and external entrapment. Part of her entrapment is a social narrative that she is committed to, which defines the normalcy and normativeness of growing up in a normal family. The result is alienation and a sense that her life is directed by forces beyond her control. Her need to be normal and conform to "them" comes at the expense of giving up on herself. Her existential efforts were directed mostly at attempts to reaffirm that her existential space belongs to her. Paradoxically, efforts to control this dynamic end up limiting it. This gains visibility when an intimate relationship becomes a real possibility and an opportunity to redefine herself and the story of her life. The dilemma Ortal faces is between adjustment as experienced throughout her life and breaking through it with authenticity to overcome continued bad faith.

The second case illustration

The next case illustrates the dilemma between death and lack of authenticity. Isaac, 53, is divorced and the father of two adult children. He works as a physiotherapist. He started coughing and was treated with a syrup that produced partial results. The cough continued, he lost weight, experienced shortness of breath and weakness, and was finally referred to x-rays. The diagnosis was cancer of the throat. After surgery he began chemotherapy and radiation. At some point, he had to quit his job. Throughout the discovery of the illness and the initial stages of treatment, Isaac kept things to himself and did not reveal his situation. He was afraid of causing pain for his parents, of the stigma of being a cancer patient, and of being abandoned by friends because of the prejudices related to the illness. With the encouragement of the social worker, he revealed the illness to his parents. When lung cancer was discovered, he moved to his parents' home. His parents helped him physically and emotionally, as much as they could, particularly his father. His mother was an introverted person who helped a great deal with his basic needs, but his interactions with her were limited to daily activities and the symptoms of the illness. Isaak felt alone and misunderstood. He felt that no one could share his experience and was incapable of expressing feelings. In his relationships with others, he talked very little about his illness and stated that he didn't like others feeling sorry for him. Other people's pity made him much embarrassed and discomfited in his interactions. He gradually cut himself off from friends and significant others. In his talks with the social worker, he kept to the illness and ascribed it to causes unrelated to his choices, such as genetic history. He described others' reactions to his illness as social injustice. We can interpret Isaak's illness as biographic discontinuity, him being in need of integrative meaning in the context of his overall life story (Carel, 2008). The cancer patient needs to find an explanation for his suffering and for the limits imposed on him, for the implications of the illness for his choices concerning relationships, and for the ways of going about his life. He needs to face the dilemma of what to give up of his previous identity. He must develop a different approach to his temporality and to his relationship with the present and the future in the presence of the impending death.

For Heidegger (1927/1996), the tension between authentic and inauthentic life is due to people's relation to their own finitude. Regarding this statement by Heidegger, Mulhall (1996) wrote that confronting death is associated with significant consequences:

> First, it makes Dasein aware of itself as the kind of being for whom its own Being is an issue: the fact that death is perceived as threatening shows that Dasein's existence matters to it. Second, it forces Dasein to acknowledge that what matters to it about its existence is not just the specific moments that make it up, but the totality of those moments; in acknowledging death as a threat not just to some particular possibility of its Being but to its Being as such, Dasein acknowledges that what is an issue for It is not just any given moment of its life but its life as a whole. It thereby comes to see that its life is something for which it is responsible, that its life is its own to live. This, however, leads to the third consequence, since it is also forced to admit that typically his life is in the hands of the others, lived out in the terms established by the 'they' rather than those which are close to its own individuality.

(119)

To bring these abstract philosophical statements down to earth, we illustrate them with Isaac's case. The insight that he is vulnerable because he cannot escape his own death provokes anxiety together with the tendency to deny it. He is faced with the need to examine his life as a whole, his relationships with others, his parents and others he took for granted. We must point to two existential states experienced by individuals in these situations. One is "forgetfulness of being" (Mulhall, 1996), which relates to an unauthentic "lifeworld" immersed in small and non-significant life events, trivia, without ongoing awareness of one's responsibility for one's life. This goes along with denial of freedom. Isaac described his life before his illness as emotionally disconnected, a state that became stronger after his divorce. He found himself alone, without an active social life, alone with his computer after working hours. He further described a constant race after financial security and a higher standard of living, which made him neglect his values and by and large lose his commitment to his profession and his life. The outcome was that he felt haunted by a lack of meaning in life. Bad faith emerged as a leitmotif, further escalating his alienation from choice and responsibility and his perception that life depends on others who are strange and hostile. Following the discovery of illness, the nothingness became associated with impending death and the absence of something positive to look forward to taking over his existence.

The second state is "mindfulness of being" (Mulhall, 1996), representing authenticity. In a state of mindfulness of being, we are aware of the possibility of forgetfulness of being, automatic existence, and dissatisfaction. We are aware that we are the source of self-limitation and not of some external reality, show our willingness to fight bad faith, and assume responsibility for our possibilities and choices. The movement from a state of forgetfulness to one of mindfulness and authenticity is not always dependent on us, and may arise from a high-level upheaval that undermines the foundations of forgetfulness of being. Fear of impending death is the most unsettling situation. For Isaac, authenticity is being-toward-death (Heidegger, 1927/1996).

In sum, we must bear in mind that the two modes, authenticity and inauthenticity, are structurally grounded in Dasein and create unity (Golomb, 1995) through a dialectical dynamic. Thus, without inauthenticity there is no authenticity and *vice versa*. Therefore, what is authentic is subjective, and there may be differences based on various existential situations, thus we can speak about the human struggle to become authentic rather than about given authentic character. van Deurzen-Smith (1997) formulated the Heideggerian view of authenticity as a struggle to better understand the inevitable connections to the world. In Sartre's view, an authentic person is aware of oneself, one's relation to the world and others, makes choices and actions that transcend one's freedom within the limits of facticity (Daigle, 2011; Golomb, 1995). Thus authenticity is seen as an ongoing challenge rather than a one-time occurrence. Existentialists emphasize being true to oneself and not looking for the real self because the self is not a pre-determined, fixed, and static entity, but rather a process (Pollard, 2005). It is reasonable to say therefore that authenticity is the result of an ever-changing attitude toward the self and the world.

4 Being with and among others

From an existential standpoint, being in the world is always relational (Cohn, 1997; Spinelli, 2007). The basis of relatedness involves being conscious of the mutuality between the self and others, including "being-with-others" while being oriented toward "others" and recognizing that we are conscious of this; and experiencing existence as the situation of the other, associated with the recognition that the self exists in relation with others and their perspectives of us. From an existential standpoint, there is no **me** without **you**.

The following case description demonstrates the dynamic of being with others in constructing the self. Steve, 42, is divorced, father of two children from two different mothers, an addict since his 20s, returned to the therapeutic community for substance and alcohol abuse, where he had been treated 10 years earlier. In the last 10 years, he was able to stay clear of drugs, and was functioning normatively for a year and a half. His recent referral followed detention for drug trafficking, and treatment was an alternative to incarceration. He described it as follows: "I was in this room 10 years ago with another social worker. During my last incarceration, my family pressured me to return to the therapeutic community. I refused at first, thinking I prefer to do my time and get it over with. But following some conversations with other inmates, I decided to come back and work on issues which I didn't the last time." To the social worker's question about what he thought he had not worked on last time he answered: "My problem is that I don't know who I am. What kind of person I am. Bad? Good? Capable of a total failure? Strong, weak, brave, coward? I don't know why I can't stay clean. Why do I keep ruining what I build?"

In response to the social worker's probing, Steve described conflicting voices coming from within, each one arguing against the other that it is unauthentic, fake, and disguised. He asked the social worker: "Help me find out who the real Stevie is. Help me learn, accept, and like myself, and understand what brings me back to dope." The therapeutic relationship revealed that the contradictory voices are expressions

DOI: 10.4324/9781003322085-5

of others' perception of him, particularly in his relationships with his mother and father, his failure to meet expectations, their perception of him as weak and failing, vis-à-vis their expectation that he become a source of pride and support for them. His experience was one of suffering, constant movement between the desire to make it and the shame of not succeeding. One of the recurring themes in his narrative was that his parents did not allow him to play with his peers in the neighborhood, which was a disadvantaged and crime-ridden area. He recalled how he watched from the window other children playing, without being able to participate. He further recalled his mother secretly asking an older nephew to take care of him in school because he is too weak to defend himself. He remembered this as humiliating, and it filled him with anger. As a reaction to it, he always picked fights with stronger children to validate his strength and his courage. Although he was willing to pay the price of pain and injury to prove his strength to his mother, she continued viewing him as a vulnerable victim. This is a vivid illustration of being in the world through intentionality toward specific others who define who one is.

People are thrown into interpersonal relationships and, dialectically speaking, being becomes *with* or *in resistance to* others (Tillich, 1952/1966). Existentialists are divided on the issue of relations of self to others. One approach maintains that interpersonal relationships are based on threatening mutuality, focusing on the danger that the other has the power to construct the other's being (his/her identity) as object (e.g., stigmatize). This gives the other the strength to deny the freedom one possesses about one's existence in the world. (e.g., Sartre, Heidegger, Laing). The other approach (Buber, Levinas) regards existence with others as a path to potentially ethical being as salvation resulting from dialogue. The self in relation to others is drawn outside itself by the other's existence. The opportunity to perceive the positioned-self vis-à-vis "thou" as a unique face is central to human existence. In this process, the self is called upon to recognize human suffering, stop faking, and unveil itself. The intersubjective approach underlying such a perspective is made possible when the self can connect to the other while recognizing the limitations, asymmetry, and mutuality arising from me being me and the other as other, different, and absolutely outside the self.

The other as a threat

Sartre (1943/1966) maintained that the self is immersed in "the look" (le regard) of the others and becomes the object of intentions and judgments. The self-image is constituted from outside reflections of the self in the other's view. Any situation of the individual as object is experienced as alienating, denying, and labeling. The basic experience of self is one of entrapment in the perspective of the other (Reynolds, 2006). By internalizing the self as perceived by others, it becomes dependent, as the self is in need of existential feedback, which determines its self-image. The other becomes a key factor in the creation of self-consciousness, which is experienced as loss of freedom and a forcible limitation (Daigle, 2010). In the course of such dynamics, anguish, the product of bad faith, eventually distorts the interaction with others and leads to renouncing one's authenticity (Webber, 2009). In these situations, the self perceives others as imposing fixed traits on it, the reaction to which is to attribute these traits to others. The experience is a sense of deprivation, distress, and confrontation with others. The ensuing anxiety, as an underlying trait of existing with others, is dramatically expressed in Sartre's dictum, "Hell is other people" (*L'enfer, c'est les autres*, No Exit; 1949). The three protagonists in Hell had no mirrors. Common to their experience was the need for others so that they can receive validation for their selves, as they perceived themselves. The power of others to define them was experienced as hell.

Stevie's story reflects the experience of lack of freedom in being and choosing, while the judgment of others defines his existential experience. His choice of behaviors under "the look" of others is supposed to reflect to him who he is. The result is an experience of a split, of pain, and of lack of authenticity. In his existential conflict, Stevie moves between a wish to be defined as normative. but he is weakened by his expectation that others view him as strong. His conduct makes him feel fake in his own eyes and in that of others. His power arises from his entanglement in deviance and from his conflicts with law enforcement. Detention removes him from the normative path, which he perceives as weakening him.

The family is the mutual perceptions of self and others in all possible variations. This social unit unveils and weaves together individual narratives and biographies, together with the resulting interpretations and unique meanings attributed to events, relationships, and reflective processes. Children learn early to position themselves within the interpretations and reflections framing them in relations with others. Families produce joint linguistic preferences, meanings, and interpretations needed to construct reality. The sense of belonging and *we*-ness at the basis of the ontological security of family members can also be used to control, hurt, and threaten them. Similar processes can be identified in meaningful organizations in which individuals participate, such as schools, workplaces, and so on.

The look of shame

Sartre's metaphor for interpersonal processes is expressed by the term "the look" (Sartre, 1943/1966). According to him, the phenomenological revelation of existence with the others is affected by their mere presence: the ontological other reveals the structure of our existential experiences, together with the others' attitude toward us (Webber, 2011). In Sartre's view, the other's look is at odds with one's experience of one's self in the world. Therefore, the main experience of the other is terrifying, and the self seeks to defend itself by attempting to control the look, thereby minimizing its influence on identity. Such relationships are by definition conflictual, and the central concern in these situations is that the individual becomes objectified. A possible way out is to objectify the other, a dynamic in which the central emotion is "shame" (Sartre, 1943/1966). To understand this experience, we must distinguish between guilt and shame. Common to both emotions is the focus on the gap between the desirable and socially permissible on one hand, and the deviant and forbidden on the other. Both emotions lead to negative self-perception. Guilt leads us to focus on our deficiencies and mistakes, but admits the possibility of forgiveness, repair, and compensation, including punishment. Such modes of restoration, both actual and symbolic, represent familiar social codes for repair and can help us experience the self and others' acceptance. By contrast, in shame, the self is perceived as lacking value and as useless. The result is an experience of failure and a sense of defectiveness and entrapment with no way out. Zahavi (2011) summarized this dynamic as follows: "To feel shame is—if ever so fleetingly—to accept the other's evaluation; it is to acknowledge that I am that object that the other looks at and judges" (p. 216). The result is an experience of rejection by the self and others; we feel powerless, lose control, and overall minimized in the eyes of others. The experience of shame means that our deeds are bad, and the self is as bad as its deeds. Shame is deep, hidden, masked, and slippery. People fail to verbalize it, yet its presence is destructive for the self, and there is a tendency to avoid experiencing and knowing it.

The self is other-dependent to actualize existence (Webber, 2009). Laing (1960) talked about being in the world in such a position of ontological insecurity. According to Laing, ontological security is the fundamental experience of the self in relation to life events, based on a clear sense of reality and self-identity, together with the reality of the other's existence. That is to say, we live with a sense of autonomy and boundaries separating us from others, with continuity in time and with the same body in various spaces, well known to others. In experiencing ontological insecurity, we acquire a sense of uncertainty about knowing our own identity, which we can no longer experience without being over-sensitive to time, space, and others. Thus, life events are experienced as threats to the identity. The ontologically insecure individual is incapable of experiencing either connection to others or disconnection from them. In relations with others, one self-sacrifices authenticity to avoid ontological insecurity and gain a false security. A dichotomy emerges between the real and false self. The paradox lies in the inability of the self to communicate with others, while the other is nested within the self and can deny the entire process ontologically. The other has the power to deny the freedom and authenticity of the other self. Under such conditions, the existential experience is controlled by anxiety and fear of nothingness, leading to the abyss of loss of meaning (Tillich, 1952/1966). The anxiety is paralyzing, and the paralysis helps control anxiety through minimization and denial, side-tracking and marginalizing. The sense of lack of autonomy gives birth to a need for outside order to identify paralysis and act to overcome it, resulting in conformity and obedience to "generalized others" or "they." In the final analysis, Stevie's case attests to a sense of loss of autonomy, which threatens the self. He is trapped in the view of others, who have the power to make him anxious and experience ontological insecurity. They can both confine and release him, which makes his existence threatening.

Another way of understanding the dynamics of alienation from an interpersonal world is by Frankl's concept of "existential vacuum" (1969/1988). The sense of lack of authenticity and the inability to rely on the self and on the interpersonal world results in a lack of positive existential orientation, of a sense of commitment. It produces an experience of uprootedness from the ability to experience the commitment of others, in particular of significant others. In the absence of inner sources of meaning, the individual turns to outer sources to avoid the existential vacuum. This is a false state. For example, the use of drugs is the result of a lack of meaning in life, which provides a pseudo-defense against existential vacuum, but in reality, reinforces the state it tries to evade.

The second perspective: The other as an opportunity for dialogue

At the heart of this approach is the assumption that as individuals we cannot fully experience our being by ourselves without another self being present (Buber, 1923/2000). Individuals do not carry within themselves their own subjectivity, which emerges only in relation to others, through dialogue. "The meaning of this dialogue is found in neither one nor the other of the partners, nor in both taken together, but in their interchange" (Friedman, 2002, p. 98). The distinction between Sartre and Buber lies in the fact that Sartre perceived the other as an obstacle on the road to freedom, and thought that the individual must dispose of the other's objectifying look. By contrast, for Buber the other means freedom. Buber differentiated between I-It and I-Thou. Both are basic existential notions, expressing the existence of self. In I-It, the other is viewed as an object, whereas in I-Thou, there is space for the subjectivity of the self and of the other. The transformation of the self occurs in both ways. In I-It, the self is encapsulated, alienated, and objectified.

In I-Thou, the self actualizes its subjectivity with relationship to the social world. Buber recognized that both paths are needed for existence, but I-Thou is the preferred relational option. For example, when a social worker deals with a cancer patient to achieve specific goals, such as realizing the patient's rights vis-à-vis the National Insurance Institute, the social worker uses the I-It pattern. But when attempting to experience the other's fear and pain in depth, there is no alternative to I-Thou. When I address the other from the I-It mode of being, I am searching and analyzing the other while relating to a specific aspect of that person's existence; therefore, my self exists only partially. As a result, there is no encounter. By contrast, in I-Thou, the self approaches the world and the other from a position of openness, with a total view of the self and the other. The outcome is a fusion in the encounter, willingness, and readiness to experience an entity that was not previously conceived. Buber used the concept of confirmation of the other. Confirmation is the full acceptance of the other. Through confirmation, relationships become based on inclusion, that is, the ability to simultaneously develop a sense of willingness to enter into a dialogue, a sense of self, and a sense of the other. What is involved in the inclusion process is the full presence of the other, without giving up on the inclusion of the self. In the relational sense, when in a state of I-Thou, we relate to the present, including that which is emerging. The inclusion process comes to life when the other recognizes the self in its integrity and uniqueness.

Buber avoided an explicit conceptualization and used poetic language, charged with questions and meanings. But his belief was based on the idea that existence emerges through dialogue, and that anything significant emerges as dialogical. Through dialogue, a new ontological reality is revealed. Buber emphasized that there is a need to be ready to perceive the other and recognize that the other is communicating and trying to direct something at the other. One needs to accept the role of recipient and work on establishing a dialogue. Being a recipient often means giving up one's standard behavioral patterns, talking less about oneself or trying to engender something specific. It means giving up "seeming" (appearances) and unveiling the self in its fullness and authenticity.

According to Levinas (1947/1987, 1961/1969), Western philosophy failed to view the other as a distinctive entity. Otherness is viewed as interfering, and consequently there is a tendency to dismiss it. The other is perceived as temporarily part of the self. Its dismissal is accomplished by annexing the other to the self on the basis of sameness. This enables relationships based on totality. It starts from an external position, in which the self becomes a theoretical spectator, using meta-categories to understand and know the other (Kunz, 2002). A salient example of this is the development of diagnostic categories that define the other based on apparently extrinsic information. Yet such categorization contains the other in the totality of the categories we, as professionals, create of the other.

Levinas believed that existence can be understood only in ethical terms in relation to others. This is contrary to the dominant belief that existence starts from the self and acts outward (Large, 2015). Levinas uses the concept of "infinity" to illustrate his ethical position that the other is always beyond totality and categorization. In his view, the self is involved in relating to the other as subject, from a position of infinite responsibility (ethical focus). The other is perceived as being outside the boundaries, abilities, and powers of the self, and as such beyond its reach. The other attempts to establish a model of relationships with the self, which respects its foreignness and preserves otherness in its totality. Otherness for Levinas is an event rather than some specific entity. The other is neither the discovery nor the reflection of the self, including previous acquaintance or history, and it is not caused by the meaning provided by the self. The other enters the world of the self without permission, without any consideration of the dimensions of the self, without considering the willingness or the capacity of the self. The initiative of unveiling the other does not belong to the self but to the other, and as such, it involves its reaction and answers. Sagi (2018) said that "Levinas's other is not a concrete being, a real other, but a presence of transcendence" (p. 132).

This transcendence depends on the ability of the self "to envision the face" (Levinas's term for the other being), which the self does not perceive as a collection of visual effects but rather as expressions of how others present themselves to the self, departing from the self-perception of the others (Morgan, 2011). "The face" of the other demolishes the individual's ability to preserve an objective knowledge of the other and include the other as part of the view of the self. In the encounter, the other confronts the self with a consciousness related to the unlimited possibilities of the other, which are beyond one's knowledge and understanding. The face presents the vulnerability of the other, its destitution, and yet reflects responsibility with respect to the demands of the other from the self (Kuntz, 2002).

Levinas's ethics can be illustrated by a case that is commonly defined in social work as a "multi-problem family." Liz, 33, is married to David, a released offender. She has two children, a boy of 12 and a girl of 7. The children are from a previous relationship with a Muslim man with whom she was entangled since she was 12. Her son was diagnosed with attention deficit disorder (ADD). He has violent outbursts in school and at home, including violence against his mother. At the time of the intervention neither partner worked, and their only income was from welfare and social security. Liz's parents were drug addicts, deeply involved in the criminal world. They divorced when she was in her early adolescence, and she was brought up by her grandmother. At the time when her father was imprisoned, she started her relationship with the Muslim man, who was a drug dealer and an addict. Liz cut off her relationship with her mother in anger, and never forgave her for neglecting her. She retained the connection to her father, who remarried, quit drugs, had a job, and led a normative life. In her welfare file, Liz is described as part of a multigenerational multi-problem family: she was born into one and was creating another one. She was submissive, tended to have problematic heterosexual relationships with antisocial men, neglected her children's needs, and reacted with hostility to social workers and educators of her children in school. She was referred to treatment at a center for family therapy because of her problems with her children. She described a struggle for economic survival, experienced loneliness, viewed herself as a single mother with no support of any kind from her husband, unable to set boundaries for her older boy, and felt misunderstood by school authorities. She also describes a sense of threat arising from the identity problems of her children who were born to a Jewish mother and a Muslim father. Both she and her children continued to hide these facts and expressed fear of the day when this would become known. From Levinas's perspective, the social worker is expected to see "the face of the other" as an expression of ethical responsibility. This implies hearing Liz's narrative and being committed to it from within her existential experience, while confronting it with the biographic facts, the diagnostic and clinical rationale, and with the professional discourse, values, and emotions of the social worker. It also implies making the meetings with Liz a "presence of transcendence," overcoming fear and risk, and being ready to initiate a dialogue in which Liz is understood in her wholeness, generating meanings that involve values, strengths, and competencies, together with positive intentionality toward her children. The meaning of responsibility in this case is listening to Liz being in the world and recognizing her key strength arising from the fact that she was never involved in the criminal world and never used drugs.

This case illustrates Levinas's concept of "ethical resistance," which is essentially a question mark related to the power and freedom of the self vis-à-vis the presence of the other. The ethical relation, as presented by Levinas, is the challenge involved in the presence of the other. The perspective of the other brings about responsibility by the self. Such responsibility exists independently of whether the self accepts or rejects it, whether the self is or is not knowledgeable about how to activate it, and whether the self can act on behalf of the other in any concrete way. Levinas did not equate the rights of the self and others in producing dialogue. Rather, he used a language of the obligation of the self, which enables and demands dialogue. The implication is that the dialogue is actualized at the ethical level. Such a level of the relationship involves recognition of the freedom of the other and commitment to the responsibility to preserve that freedom. Levinas's responsibility departs from Sartre's perspective on the issue of whether individuals are condemned to be free. Levinas demands going beyond freedom, to doubt the freedom of the self and renounce individual interests, while emphasizing responsibility toward others.

Common to Buber and Levinas is the subjective perception of the relationship to the other as an expression of being in the world. Levinas recognized Buber's emphasis on dialogue as the center of existence but criticized his use of the term "Thou." In his view, Buber's use of the term leads the other into a relationship based on mutuality, in which language enables the minimization of the symbolic distance and creates a partnership. In Buber's mutuality, the other loses its absolute character, making such mutuality impossible from Levinas's perspective. For Buber, the purpose of dialogue is the creation of a unified partnership based on common denominators and co-participation. For Levinas, the relationship between I and Thou is based on facing the outsideness of the other, which is radically different from the self. An ethical dialogue for Levinas is one based on difference rather than similarity and oneness. The other turns to the self with demands and expectations and asks for answers. The face of the other is screaming, demanding and constantly reminding us of the *a priori* responsibility assumed by the self, which is not the result of anything from the past or previous acts and choices. The possibility of denying responsibility is inherent in the encounter with the other.

Case illustration

To demonstrate the complexities involved in the foregoing discussion, we use the example of a social work intervention, carried out by a social worker working at a center for children at risk. The client is the Levy family. Galina, 59 years old, is the grandmother of Dana, a 10-year-old girl. Dana's parents are diagnosed as retarded and as such unable to care for her. The grandmother Galina has been taking care of Dana ever since she was born, and is bringing her up as her own daughter. Dana was removed from the grandmother's home legally because of suspicions of sexual abuse by Galina's partner (not her biological grandfather). The intervention process included emotional therapy for Dana, and social work treatment for Galina. The intervention was presented to Galina as an imposed precondition for considering the possibility of the child returning to her home. Galina came to the treatment with heavy guilt feelings and anger concerning the removal of the grandchild from her home. She was ashamed of being accused of not protecting her grandchild. She told the social worker that Dana was removed from the home because of abuse in school, and she stated that she believed the teacher was beating her. She repeatedly reasserted her love for Dana, who entered her life as a beam of light, bringing happiness to her. Galina stated that she was happy to take on the parental role for Dana, without any hesitation, from the onset. The social worker at the Center tended to believe that Galina was incapable of facing the issues in her life directly, and developed denial mechanisms and projections of blame upon others. Her diagnosis was further validated by the child protection worker in the social service department, describing extreme neglect, failure in parenting competencies, and lack of responsibility toward the child. Moreover, the social worker could not believe Galina's stories in the light of the accumulated evidence regarding the sexual abuse of her granddaughter, and Galina's subsequent neglect and malfunctioning as a parental figure. The social worker realized that for the therapeutic intervention to succeed, she must connect with Galina's world, or the therapeutic intervention will be meaningless. The social worker felt she needed to take a position either for or against Galina, and these positions were irreconcilable: one was based on a professional view, from the outside, and the other based on Galina's stories, from the inside. The social worker needed to introduce order into the narrative, decide who is against whom, who were the bad guys and the good guys, and who was responsible for dealing with various issues. She felt that organizing Galina's world in a manner that presented it as pathological, dishonest, and malfunctioning would help her blame Galina for failing to protect the granddaughter. This perception follows the theoretical orientation that children experiencing abuse always grow up in dysfunctional families, and that children growing up in such families and still preserving positive feelings toward the family have a distorted view of the world.

Analyzing this dynamic shows that the look, in Sartre's sense, from both sides of the gap, was one of mutual denial of the other's subjectivity and freedom. The sense of being-for-others results in anxiety, shame, and mutual powerlessness. From the grandmother's point of view, the social worker has the power to define her as an object in the world; she strips her identity in the eyes of others, including judges, police, and sundry players in the social welfare establishment. Galina perceives that the social worker is robbing her of her fundamental project as a grandparent. Both feel that they are not able to affect each other's perceptions.

Initially, the social worker failed to realize that transforming the grandmother into a diagnosis, a stigmatized, negative image, is part of the grandmother's consciousness about social services and social workers. The social worker truly views the grandmother's self as pathological, inauthentic, and false (resistant), and she denies the possibility that the grandmother's false self is a result of attempts to deal with the prevalent narrative created by the social workers themselves. The conflict was rooted in the I-It ontological gap, with both Galina and the social worker attempting to increase the ontological insecurity of the other. The social worker casts doubt on Galina's love and care for her granddaughter; Galina questions the moral and legal right of social workers as agents protecting the child. The social worker, with power differential to her advantage, presents herself as a crusader for children's wellbeing and protector of the child, continuing the I-It relationship.

The social worker's sense of positive professional being in the world is substantiated and supported by the narratives of the welfare system professionals, which emphasize a view of clients as neglecting and abusive parents, of a fixed nature. The parents are seen as lacking motivation and responsibility, and being manipulative, dishonest, and unreliable. This makes it possible for the social worker to suppress hard, contradictory, and difficult feelings, and to regard "the lady" sitting across from her as unworthy of bringing up her granddaughter. The accepted professional expectation is for the client to accept the diagnosis, assessment, and stigmatization. In the course of such dynamics, the personal and the social-professional narratives disempower the I-Thou relationship. Reflecting on one's being-with-others as existential freedom produces anxiety. Therefore, the temptation to activate bad faith is strong. Everything is pointing in the direction of ending the custody of the grandmother.

As the therapeutic process progresses, the social worker becomes increasingly persuaded that her position about Galina's incompetence as a parental figure contradicts her professional need to establish an interpersonal relationship, connect to the client's world, and create an alliance that enables her to identify the strengths and abilities that are a precondition for change. When the social worker comes to realize this reality concerning Galina, a new kind of relationship begins, aimed at discovering who is Galina, attempting to connect with her and understand her experience in the world and her "fundamental project." Such understanding of the role of the social worker involves renouncing the early assumptions about Galina, remaining open, and allowing for an experience of vagueness, rife with the unknown, which threatens the social worker's professional identity.

In Levinas's terms, the relationship toward the other becomes absolute and arises from the ethical recognition that the other being, and is reflected in the face of Galina. Galina's face calls for transcendence. From this perspective, the grandmother is seen as an ethical challenge, and not as an irresponsible liar, which is how she is presented by outside sources, or as a loving individual caring for her granddaughter, as Galina seeks to present herself. Instead, she is a collection of occurrences that shaped her into what she is, complex and multifaceted, waiting for the social worker to reveal her. The minute such an understanding is in place, the social worker perceives her work as a journey into understanding who Galina is, her experience in the world, and her fundamental project. The social worker seeks to answer questions such as what creates the unity between Galina's past, present, and future, and how to identify the meaningful themes in her life. This view has a transformative effect and brings a judgmental to a committed reflective stance. It serves as an empowering force for both Galina and Dana, making possible a mutual alliance between them. It enables, in turn, dealing with Dana's return home, or alternatively, with her placement in a residential setting. From Buber's perspective, the encounter of the social worker with the grandmother marks a crossroads between two individuals who share the challenge to transform each other from objects into subjects. For the social worker, the encounter with Galina creates an ethical commitment to abandon earlier assumptions about her, and to stay within the boundaries of a limited and unclear space in which everything is open and nothing is clear and known. This is associated with viewing the world as disorderly and confusing, lacking meaning, and threatening the sense of competence of the social worker. Such dynamics reflect situations in which social workers in child welfare and various other social agencies face the need to actualize the ethical challenge inherent in the I-Thou (otherness), which clashes with the I-It demand, that is, the pressure to diagnose, assess dangerousness or risk, and exercise additional forms of social control.

Buber's distinction between *being* and *seeing* is a useful heuristic device for examining the social worker's attitude and activity. In *being*, the social worker needs to renounce concern with the ways she is perceived by others ("What should the good social worker do?") and be focused on the being of Galina as an expression of existential threat. Being attuned to the otherness of the grandmother involves unconditional commitment and responsibility, denying the social worker the option of choosing from other possibilities.

To summarize being-with-others, we can use two seemingly opposed paradoxical mottos: One is that "I started to live the day I stopped giving account to other people" vis-à-vis "I started to live the day I began giving account to other people." Our existence reflects the tension between these two poles. Wisdom lies in knowing on which side to be when, where, and with whom, for what purpose. The challenge is in the simultaneous presence of the two extremes. Social workers must cope with people stuck at one of them, struggling with social and psychological realities, without considering the deeper consequences of being at one end or the other. Others represent both a threat and an ethical challenge.

Social work clients experience mostly anxiety as the dominant dimension of being with others and fail to address the challenges inherent in these situations. The key to the challenge of social work is the ability to transform the anxiety toward each other into an opportunity for self-reflection and by doing so, to gain a deeper understanding of the situation on both sides.

5 Being in time

One can make sense of being in the world and experience it only within the boundaries of time (Adams, 2018; Spinelli, 2007). Being conscious about time from an existential perspective is chronological (growing old) and mostly experiential, reflecting our relationship with the world (Cox, 2009). From an existential-phenomenological standpoint, there is a difference between clock time and lived time. Time is not an outcome of specific causal systems but rather the result of the way one lives in the world. The deepest human experiences such as anxiety, depression, and happiness occur in time and space, yet people report their experiences mostly in time (May, 1983). For instance, persons with depression or severely ill feel that their situation destroys their future; rape victims may feel that time freezes at the moment of the occurrence of rape; persons losing control over memory in time (such as Alzheimer's patients) lose their identity. According to Heidegger, being outside time is being thrown into meaninglessness.

In constructing a narrative of our life, we never know ahead of time what will happen (e.g., when will we die). This is the result of our being in the world, and it combines certainty and uncertainty, hope and disillusionment, expectations, wishes, and facts. The only guaranteed finitude is our death (Yalom, 2008). We become aware of the passing of time and of how it affects our being by its effect on our body and physical being. We compare pictures of the way we looked over time, always in the context of our being in the world. Our relation to time is colored by whether time is on our side or against us. We hope time will be merciful to us and we will not become ill or demented. The metaphoric expression of time reflects this existential connection to lived time. This is an ontological experience, and it should be distinguished from the ontic experiences of everydayness (Adams, 2018).

The perception of time as existential coherence

Existential thinking about time is paradoxical: time is chronological, yet this order is not based merely on logical rationality but depends on one's

DOI: 10.4324/9781003322085-6

Dasein (Hoffman, 1986). Individuals can feel that they are out of time. This sense of time is evident in people in total institutions such as prisons or mental hospitals, when life stops and time becomes meaningless. Time is a collection of constructed temporary experiences, which have no distinguishable form but a circular structure, in which the past is simultaneously holding the present and the future, and the future is simultaneously holding both the past and the present (Spinelli, 2007). Individuals examine and imagine the future from a perspective of how the present will affect it. Creating a pessimistic or optimistic image of the future contains the possibility of existential guilt and regret because it involves an inherent potential for threat, failure, and disaster.

Chronological time is not what is existentially important according to Richardson (2012): "What's at issue here are not future, past and present 'themselves,' but our intentional stance towards them" (p. 181). From such a perspective, existence is simultaneously open to the past, present, and future. Existentially, we are a set of possibilities in time (Webber, 2009). The future is the preferred dimension because ontologically speaking, the past and the present are embodied in the future. Thus "the future *destabilizes* the present" (Hoffman, 1986, p. 92) and we exist within the "what if . . . then" questions. In social work with abused women, when questions arise concerning divorce, separation, reporting to the police, or getting a restraining order, existential meaning exists within the constraints of time and possibilities: What will happen if . . . ? Some do nothing because they are busy calculating the effect in time of their behavior on their children. Such calculation is tied to the ontological experience involving values, emotions, worldview, societal reaction, and cultural context.

As Sartre described it (1943/1966), the existential experience of time is located in the paradox of human reality inherent in the statements "no longer" and "not yet." Therefore, at any moment, the individual can be defined only as a projection, a subject directed toward the future. The future is needed as a projection of our existence, and as such, it is always missing. Cox (2009) maintained that "the present is simply the presence of consciousness to the world as a being that constantly transcends the past towards the future" (p. 33). What individuals remember as significant life events depends on the decision regarding the possibilities the future holds in the present moment (May, 1958, 1983; van Deurzen & Adams, 2011).

The following case histories illustrate time-related issues in existential social work.

Case illustration

Suzi is a 36-year-old single woman. She met the social worker at the Center for Single Parents, whom she came to consult about the possibility of having a child out of wedlock. She said that she would have preferred to marry but could not find an appropriate partner. She felt that her biological clock was ticking, and that she was running out of time. She described in detail her need and motivation to bring a child into the world and become a mother, but at the same time she experienced various fears and doubts: Could she handle such a heavy commitment alone? What is the right thing to do, bringing up a child alone, with no family? Will the satisfaction she gets from her work (she was a senior accountant), her hobbies, and her social life be sufficient for her without a family? Will she be able to provide for the child's needs, which usually takes two parents to do? Will she have social support and recognition for her decision? Will her decision to bring up a child without a father be moral with respect to the child? Is there meaning to existence without a child of your own?

This is an example of being as a projection into the future. In a Sartrean sense, the first issue has to do with Suzi's fundamental project. Her choice totalizes her being. Her questions and dilemmas are personal and unique. Other women may perceive the future without questioning it and take it for granted.

The second issue emerging from this case is that the experience of time is mostly ontological. Suzi is projecting into the future decisions that need to be taken now and that will define her life. The question that remains to be answered has to do with her being in the world. What is the meaning of Suzy's life? Will things work out according to her wishes or will she run into difficulties? The present time is experienced as lacking the possibility of active and meaningful choice and action.

Third, meaning cannot be examined without recognizing the anxiety involved. Suzi's anxiety is connected with a strong feeling of discontent about not having accomplished something in her life that is critical to her being. There is something she did not clarify for herself during her life. She focuses on fears and attempts to evade the experience of anxiety. The fear arising from the question of whether she can meet the child's needs for both parents can be solved based on research-based knowledge and technical answers. The question of whether existence is meaningful without children of one's own, one can answer only by facing anxiety related to being in the world, meaning, and authenticity, all nested in time. Also connected to the experience of time is the more objective dimension of biological time, which further escalates the ontological anxiety related to childbirth.

Fourth, time is bound to situation (situatedness). Suzy's experience happens within a particular time context, which includes facticity (biological time) and freedom (subjective attitude toward one's being in the world). The future is not remote, but it is the determinant condition expressed in deciding and acting in a historically situated context. There is facticity in Suzi's situation related to her life history, her social context, and the significant events in her life. These situations and givens are not opposed to her freedom. In Sartre's dialectics, freedom exists only in situations that exist through freedom (Sartre, 1943/1966). Suzy cannot not choose, but time limits her choice; there is only one choice to be realized. If the opportunity is lost, it will never be granted again. This is a classical "limit situation," located between guilt and freedom. Freedom brings about guilt. In Suzi's case, she is in the process of becoming, a narrative in the process of being written. She can give birth or not. In becoming, each option involves freedom and potential for guilt, because, as we noted repeatedly, humans live as projections in the future, without knowing how to predict the future. We often hear from clients the statement "I wish I knew . . ." in pursuit of the fantasy of controlling time and content in the future. The unique awareness of "being-in-time" has a profound effect on the way one perceives experience and acts toward the world. This further affects the temptation to act in bad faith.

Fifth, the body is a main source of existential time. Looking in the mirror and seeing the body, mostly the face, reflects one's age, evaluated as a function of time changes. Seeing the physical body may generate various emotions such as satisfaction and pride on the one hand, disappointment and disgust on the other. Others' eyes are present (concretely or symbolically) in perceiving one's body. The body reflects one's possibilities of relationships in time, as evident in Suzi's narrative. Other critical situations in which the body reflects being in time is during illness. Being sick is a present situation (diagnosis) and a projection into the future (prognosis). Both are prominent in chronic diseases, physically and mentally. It is intensive in terminal illness, when the finality of one's lived time is dominant.

Death and time

The main horror in being in time is death. Given the absoluteness of death and its effect on people, the perception and coping with death is a central concern in philosophy. In his book, *Mortal question*, Nagel (1979) formulated the issue as follows: "If death is the unequivocal and permanent end of our existence, the question arises whether it is a bad thing to die" (p. 1). This statement goes back to Socrates, who stated that people tend to present themselves as knowledgeable regarding the badness of death. Yet they know little, and therefore it is difficult to decide what is to be afraid of. For those who are seekers of wisdom, death must be feared least of all (Scarre, 2007). The Stoics and Epicureans emphasize that death is natural and cannot be defined as bad or good but needs to be viewed as the cessation of the experience rather than a goal in life. We have to fear not death but rather our judgments and representations of it. Epicurus viewed death as nothing: when a person exists death does not, and when death exists the individual does not. Thus, we cannot speak of death as something inducing harm. Therefore, the fear of death is an evil that prevents us to live a full and meaningful life. Rational thinking is suggested to overcome fear and achieve tranquility (Barry, 2007; Luper, 2009). A similar position is suggested by Spinoza, according to whom a key characteristic of the free person is following the road of wisdom, focusing on life, and giving little thought to death (Levi, 2008).

Existential theory stresses the end as a beginning point for understanding one's being and meaning at a given point in time. In the human experience of time, death is an uncontested certainty. It produces anxiety despite its certainty; therefore, people attempt to evade and deny it. The existential approach adopted the ontological view of confronting death, existential anxiety, denial, and escape from death. Heidegger emphasized that no one could die for anyone else. Everyone dies for himself. The emphasis is, therefore, on "being toward death." The Dasein is not complete without reflection on death and cannot actualize itself in fullness without such reflection. Death is challenging the individual to overcome the anxiety arising from everyday existence with *them* and achieve authenticity. Thus, being is related to actualizing the courage to be in the face of death, nonbeing, and anxiety (Tillich, 1952/1966). Whereas Heidegger analyzed the critical importance of death for liberating the individual from others, Levinas emphasized the ways in which death actualizes individual responsibility toward others.

Individuals routinely encounter death through the death of others. The younger the age, the more traumatic the event is (because it constitutes a departure from the expectations of a regular life cycle), and the broader and deeper its effect is. At some point, there is recognition that personal death is imminent, and with that recognition comes the need to face it. Children's questions about the death of their parents and their own signal a qualitative change in the experience of time. The illusion of eternal existence is shattered, and there are constant attempts by the parents to soften the certainty associated with it and to hide some of it. But even in the most secure environments and life contexts, the knowledge of impending death is present and its existential reality increases continually. Heidegger referred to "being-toward-death" as a key descriptor of being-in-time. Death is not an event but rather a way of being, an embodiment of a possible relational mode of one's being (Buben, 2015; Mulhall, 1996). Death reveals the terror of temporality of the Dasein. The strength and intensity of the ontological nature of death encourage the sense of thrownness and increase the likelihood of an unauthentic relationship with existence in time. The only way the individual can evade the temporality and the experience of death is by enslaving itself to "them," the generalized other. The defense is based on the authenticity of death, particularly on the courage involved in the recognition of possibilities and choices involved in being—toward-death (White, 2005). The recognition that death is a limit on time is critical for being in the world free of "them." The encounter with death amounts to a severe upheaval for the individual, an awakening from the illusion of temporal existence and the unveiling of the facticity of the life one needs to live. Being-toward-death involves the recognition of the totality of existence every minute, an experience-enhancing aloneness and anxiety, together with the experience of the liberation of being in time, from now to the future.

Case illustration

The following case example illustrates this dynamic. Joseph, 28, a single accounting student, is the oldest son of a family of five children. He is active and plays basketball. He was diagnosed with a malignant tumor above his knee. Until the cancer was discovered, Joseph described himself as healthy and active. He had been smoking a pack of cigarettes a day for years, never saw a doctor, and in general behaved with disregard toward his health. The illness was discovered following a series of tests he underwent at the insistence of his mother. For 6 months before the diagnosis, Joseph suffered severe pain in his leg, but despite the fact that he could barely walk after basketball games, he refused to see a doctor. Joseph reacted with indifference to the CT that identified the tumor and asked his mother not to discuss his illness with his girlfriend. Following the biopsy, the prognosis was not good because the tumor was discovered late, it was large, and had metastasized to the lungs and liver. The first stage of treatment involved hospitalization for five days of aggressive chemotherapy. The social worker began to work with him throughout and between hospitalizations.

During the first hospitalization, Joseph was a good-looking and personally pleasant man, full of humor, with a full head of hair and standard weight. At that time, he was focused on the family dynamics, his closeness to his mother, and his concern for her. He described his mother as being very verbal and overwhelming him with her talk. He described his father as a man who knew how to handle life, quite slippery, and capable of dealing with difficulties. He mentioned that at that point he was unable to listen to anyone but himself. Joseph had a tense relationship with his father, who often screamed at him, and he overheard his father talking trash to his mother. Joseph described a close relationship between the siblings and talked about solidarity in the family. The social worker witnessed this solidarity as the siblings organized being with Joseph throughout the hospitalization. Joseph described himself as being withdrawn with friends, without communication patterns in sharp contrast with observed behaviors. In his view, he had no close friends and claimed that most friendships are interest-driven. He described several long-lasting intimate relationships with women who were dependent, and only his last relationship was different because she was "a distant but independent woman." She left him immediately after the discovery of the illness. It was a difficult and sudden breakup, as she stopped coming or calling. During his first hospitalization, Joseph talked with the social worker for extended periods of time, repeatedly stating that he couldn't be angry at her, and felt sorry for her because she is expected to suffer in her life more than he did. As he described the relationship, it became evident that they never had close ties. Most of the connection was a fantasy surrounding the perfect physical looks of the girlfriend. Toward the end of the first hospitalization, Joseph began sharing with the worker his attitude toward his illness. He raised the possibility that he created his own illness as he was always closed, never shared his feelings with anyone, and the illness may be a symptom of accumulated negative feelings. He attempted to deal with the illness in a spiritual manner, read books on self-healing, and asked questions about who he was and what his relationships were with others.

By the time of the second hospitalization, Joseph was bald, had lost much weight, and his skin became yellow. At this time, he focused on himself and who he really was. He shared with the social worker a book that described the personality of someone likely to get cancer, and stated that all the details fit him. Joseph related that the book describes an individual who had no close relationships with his parents, and projected a strong outward image, without taking things to heart, whereas inward he was a sensitive person. In his view, the past is decisive and determines what happens in the present. He wanted to bring his real self forward but doubted that he could do it. He was wondering about the extent to which his real self would be acceptable to his immediate environment. Overall, Joseph felt better as treatment progressed.

During the third hospitalization, his physical condition deteriorated. He talked extensively about the meaning of life and of death. The dialogue with the social worker focused on Joseph's inability "to find a path in life." He talked about the fact that being an accountant did not suit him, and that he turned to this profession to satisfy the family's wishes. He had no idea what was suitable for him to do. He shared with the social worker that nothing truly interested him. He could not imagine the future and the freedom of choosing and changing anything. At home, he did not succeed in connecting with anyone. He did not talk to his father; friends visited less and less, and most of the time he watched basketball games on TV.

Joseph's story reflects several basic attitudes toward time and death. Existentialists maintain that death reflects the structure of consciousness and the value of space within the dimension of time. Terminal illness can cause a rupture in one's narrative. Therefore, the basic questions in understanding Joseph's Dasein are: What are the structure and quality of his relating to the present events (illness, treatments), past memories (his health), and future projections (in his words "to find a path") all within the frame of death? How can he link all time horizons into a narrative that represents his Dasein? Death accelerates the experience of time for the individual, but in trauma situations, such as facing imminent death, time slows down and freezes. Joseph attempts to create by force an experience of frozen time to avoid facing death. The taken-for-granted world is destroyed, which is reflected in his intimate relations with the family and the world in general. He seeks to avoid the consequences of experiencing the self in time. In the face of death, he focuses on attempts to preserve the past and defend himself concerning what is about to happen (basketball is a means of avoiding preoccupation with death).

Death is experienced in contrast with freedom. One's experience of freedom is blocked by the inability to do what one would want to, as before. From an existential viewpoint, death is an affirmation of freedom of choice concerning the future. The acceptance of death as the ultimate concern liberates us from losing the self in fantasies of unlimited choices. Death brings us to the recognition of limited choice in relation to the future. Following the third hospitalization, Joseph recognizes the collapse of his taken-for-granted world and begins internalizing the experience of being-toward-death. Initial attempts to evade this experience can be found in his refusal to undergo testing and his initial indifference toward the results.

Death is personal. Contrary to what is pictured in the movies, no one dies for anyone else. Thus, one needs to allow for experiencing death and its consequences on being-in-time. Joseph's need is to relate to death in the context of his life experience. Cancer, like many other chronic and terminal diseases, is a crisis in Joseph's commitment to the world. He has the option to disregard it despite its existence and continue experiencing the flow of time (bad faith); he can also fear death to the point of paralyzing and freezing life (being conquered by anxiety); or he can try to understand what death says about his life (reflective, toward authenticity).

Death reiterates the circularity of time (the future determines the past). Reflecting the knowledge of the past, death depends on an authentic understanding of the future. The meaning of suffering in the future determines the meaning of the lack of suffering in the past. In Joseph's case, the meaning of the painful treatments in the course of the illness determines the attitude toward health of one who used to be an athlete. Joseph increasingly realizes the superficial nature of his intimate relationships with women and seeks to explore a more authentic direction. Finally, death is also being-with-others.

This examination follows the dialectics of Heidegger's vs. Levinas's approaches. In Heidegger's view, one's death provides and sharpens awareness of the ever-present possibilities in constructing meaning. Impending death creates subjectivity and unveils our ability to liberate the self from others ("they"). By contrast, in Levinas's view, the effect of death on the future is one of self-liberation for the purpose of returning to the other. According to Levinas, consciousness of death does not emphasize the subject, but rather the possibility of the subject to quit the relation of the self toward the other. The death of the self, as the finality of time, hovers above the other, which is the source of the responsibility of the self. For Heidegger, death is anxiety arising from the self, facing nothingness; for Levinas, the anxiety is a connection to the future and to the others. Time and death are viewed by Levinas as intersubjective. What does this dialectic mean in understanding Joseph's being-toward-death?

Common to both Heidegger and Levinas is the belief that humans need to confront death in their being-in-time. Death unveils the subjectivity and brings about the expectation of being authentic, which in turn leads to the transformation of the individual. The recognition of subjectivity directing us to authenticity calls for affinity with external points of reference in order to enhance being. For Heidegger, this means finding values and norms that reflect authenticity; for Levinas, it means unveiling the responsibility toward the faces of the other. Self-enclosure in Heidegger's sense brings about a self-centered approach, whereas for Levinas, responsibility toward the other necessarily leads to the loss of self. According to the dialectic approach, these dimensions are interdependent because one cannot move toward others without knowing the authentic self, and cannot be an authentic self without the others. A key theme in Joseph's experience is his relationship with women. He views such relationships through the motif of physical appearance and dependence vs. independence. This view leads to a dichotomous perspective of others: either dependent or independent; either good or bad looking. These dimensions determine his past relationships with women, at the same time creating alienation toward the self and inauthenticity. He tries to figure out how others, in future encounters, will perceive him. This challenges Joseph to develop a new set of values that are not dependent upon the rigid dichotomous views that forced bad faith upon him. Death creates a time-bound crisis, making it impossible for Joseph to continue drifting in time. He needs to address authentically questions that did not preoccupy him in the past, such as who he really is (second hospitalization). Answers to these questions are a condition for him to make future encounters with women more authentic and enable him to reflect on his responsibility toward others. All of this is contingent on his present situation of being a cancer patient, recognizing that there may not be a future. By doing so, he is able to deal with the ultimate concern with death and receive the other's relation to him, while developing a sense of freedom, meaning, and choice.

6 Being in space

Together with time and others, space is a fundamental ontological dimension of being in the world. The quality of the spatial engagement determines the scope and depth of human awareness (Cohn, 1997). Narratives of life experiences are not abstractions. They are located in concrete places, occur at specific times, and involve particular participants. For example, the home space is a central existential starting point both historically and at present. Our daily experiences include places constructed as important, for which we develop attachments and therefore they become meaningful. Working spaces, for example, are such locales.

From a phenomenological perspective, existence precedes the way we know the world. Heidegger (1927/1996) stated accordingly that we need to ask how we create the space and weave it into our experiences to make them meaningful. The experience of space is highly individualized. As Ellenberger (1958) said, "[a] phenomenological analysis of oriented space must examine its component elements among which are its boundaries, right and left, distance, direction, and the vertical axis" (p. 113). Certain places may arouse a range of emotional reactions in different people. For example, some spaces may create a sense of security for some, and rejection combined with anxiety for others, depending on the intentionality involved in the meaning-making process. A good illustration of understanding the experience of space is how agoraphobia and claustrophobia create distinct meanings for different people.

The existential experience of space is further associated with the sense of relatedness and rootedness or uprootedness. Movement along this continuum becomes more acute when a crisis occurs and the taken-for-grantedness is upset. This in turn may lead to reflection over the perception of one's life narrative and self. For example, the experience of moving to a nursing home or moving as a result of divorce is associated with a sense of loss, together with the need to create meaning, and in doing so, transform the newly encountered physical space into lived space. Such events are in many ways experiential parallels to immigration. The sense of displacement and the sense that there is not much to hold on to, having no direction in space despite its physical availability,

DOI: 10.4324/9781003322085-7

is likely to lead to complex experiences of want. Struggle is involved in searching for and creating a space that provides a sense of belonging and support, and helps balance "strangerness" and alienation. In the process, one connects to space as a locale of multi-level identity change. The question "who am I?" is related to "where am I?" and "where have I been?" (Schlitte, 2017). The following case illustrates this process.

Nurith is a 59-year-old married woman, with no children because of infertility. She sought help from a social worker at the local mental health clinic for depression and continued emotional distress. Throughout the therapeutic encounters, she manifested warmth, happiness, and optimism together with openness, authenticity, curiosity, and an overall active attitude. She seemed respectful, considerate, and fair toward others. Her life story was filled with traumatic transitions. At the age of two, she lost her father. She described her mother as having violent outbursts and generally low functioning. Consequently, she was placed in foster care, where she remained for two years. From her grandmother's stories she learned that moving into foster care was quite traumatic, associated with much weeping and shock. She seemed to have serious difficulties adjusting to the new living environment. Her mother seldom visited her. When she was four, her mother remarried, and the man became her stepfather. Nurith was returned home on his initiative, as he tried to relate to her as a father. In time, a half-brother and a half-sister were born with whom she had satisfactory relationships. When Nurith was seven, the family attempted to move to a kibbutz. The experience of adjusting to kibbutz life failed repeatedly, for the entire family. When she was nine, the family returned to their previous home. The relationship with her mother became more violent, tense, and fearful, and the family's economic situation exacerbated the violence. She was removed again to her grandmother, who lived in another town, and she was expected to adjust again to a new peer group, school, and environment. When Nurith was 10, her grandmother married and Nurith was placed in residential care. She remained there until the age of 17. She was placed at times in foster families but never returned home because of the ongoing conflictual relationship with her family. At 17, she was placed against her will at another residential facility, which was expected to nurture her developmental needs and her talent for drawing and acting. The new relocation resulted in a renewed crisis. She felt lonely, insecure, and anxious about the future, and developed anorectic eating disorder that led to menopause and subsequent infertility. Two years later she returned to her mother's home again, but the destructive relationship with her had not changed. At her initiative, Nurith moved again to her grandmother's home and worked in menial jobs, experiencing spiraling loneliness and depression. She attempted suicide but was saved by her grandmother. Several months later, her grandmother passed away and Nurith was forced to return to her mother's home. At that time, she met her present husband, to whom she has been married for 39 years. She described her partner as warm, loving, giving, and intelligent. At the same time, he was jealous, treated her as his property, and like her mother, had outbursts of anger, was explosive, and tended to break objects when upset. During therapy, Nurith brought up the recurring theme of helplessness arising from the inability to make choices throughout her life, both as a child and as an adult. She kept wondering: "How could mother throw me out of the house and abandon me?" She accounted for her attempted suicides by the need to end her suffering in a future that in her experience made no sense: "I saw myself rolling on without meaning from place to place." Over months of therapy, Nurith kept repeating the mantra that she lived in a world where she was not allowed to live her way. "I was just an irrelevant creature born without a choice, born to a retarded mother who never knew what to do with me and was tossing me around . . . and me, this sort of creature, who was rolling from place to place without being asked what I wanted. I cried, I begged, I screamed, and nothing helped. What kind of freedom was that?"

The rather lengthy story of Nurith is indicative of how existential themes are located in space. One cannot deny the strong ties between the present and the memory of the spaces she lived in throughout her life. Experience that cannot be rooted in space is undefinable. Every place generates life themes, questions, and possibilities about the self. Moving from place to place produces questions of continuity of the self within one's life narrative. Nurith's life history is characterized by denial and is a collection of traumatic transitions between meaningless spaces. The way she describes the movement between spaces reflects the difficulty of achieving thematic continuity, which serves as a safety valve in one's existence. Without such continuity, the self is fragmented and vulnerable, leading to ontological insecurity (Laing, 1960). Consequently, Nurith is unable to experience what should be taken for granted: continuity and authenticity of identity. Such insecurity becomes an obstacle to achieving autonomy. Together with continuous anxiety, Nurith experiences herself as lacking the freedom to choose. Her spatial experience is temporal and unpredictable, about to explode any minute.

Metaphoric existence in space

The spatial experience is constructed through metaphors that organize and structure, and as such constitute everyday experiences. Lakoff and Johnson (1980) maintained that conceptual metaphors using the domain of space to explain and understand something that in itself is not spatial may structure one's experience in the world as spatial. One type of "metaphor we live by" is orientational, such as up/down, depth level, central/peripheral, in/out. We describe our feelings as "feeling down" or "on top of the world." Space can also define territory as broad/narrow. In this kind of spatiality, we emphasize directionality, for example, "arriving at a crossroad." Our life is often described as "finding" or "losing our way" or as the decision being "a long way off." Such metaphors situate us concretely in existential experiences with symbolic value.

The metaphors we create are never self-directed but rather point to something we strive to achieve. Natasha is 40 years old, an artist, mother of two children, and survivor of physical intimate partner violence aggravated by psychological and economic abuse. She ran away to a shelter where she stayed for several months, during which she finalized her divorce. At the first meeting at a treatment center for violence survivors, she stated the aims of her visit:

> I'd want to touch all the places that hurt me; things that bother me in life. My thoughts are always busy with this and I feel that I won't be able to get ahead if I don't leave some of these things behind me. It's not that I can possibly forget. One cannot cut off parts of one's body. It's something that will always be there. I'd love to know how I can deal with this stuff. I need to stop running away from myself.

The painful experience is represented spatially, as places where the pain is located. Some describe the pain as located in their souls, an abstract metaphoric location, which individuals must clarify for themselves in therapy. One's goals, where one wants to get, are also located in space. ("I need to move forward and leave these things behind.") The awareness that the location of pain remains unchanged makes possible continuity and a sense of coherence. The ability to project painful experiences into a symbolic or metaphoric space enables placing them in an accommodating context, which clarifies direction and provides a sense of control.

The social construction of space

A key feature of experience is the socially constructed space. One can regard these constructs as ready-made recipes of meaning, useful in interpersonal communication. Consider the ways fathers relate to visitation centers, where non-residential parents (of whom fathers are the large majority), meet their children in a professionally protected environment. The meetings are held by court order or on the recommendation of the welfare services, when unsupervised meetings may carry some type of risk, but at the same time, continued father-child relationship is in the interest of the child. One father defined the visitation center as a hostile space: "It's a prison, with cameras. The cameras are recording, all the time; you're not under normal conditions . . . Here I'm in prison, inside a room. It frustrates me. That's my most difficult experience. . . . Why do they put me in this room?! What have I done?! My daughter has feelings, too; she also understands the demeaning tone in which they speak to me, that her dad has no authority and has to ask permission for everything." The father uses the prison metaphor to describe how he experiences the world through a concept taken from another space, which he socially constructs in a manner that facilitates the communication of the experience to audiences. The use of prison as space defines the anxiety, limitations, hostility, and conflict between the keepers and the kept, similar to that between the observers and the observed. Social workers are metaphoric prison guards, control agents, who enforce laws unjustly by the use of power, with no allowance for any manifestation of autonomy or privacy. The visitation center is experienced as a locale that defines the father's identity negatively as a suspect, a source of threat, pain, shame, and social marginalization. These become a source of continued trauma and a concrete location in his struggle to survive. The result is a sense of meaninglessness, and the way to handle the resulting anxiety is to assign the meaning of being in prison. Such construction is conducive to narrative coherence. The father knows how to tell the story about the place, and doing so forces his definition upon reality. Metaphors like "prison" and "living in hell" were often used to describe degraded couple relationships. In intimate partner violence interventions, perpetrators often describe their experience as living in a prison, with the wife as a guard. The perception of the marital space as a lock-up creates and perpetuates the sense of existence as a shameful object that traps the individual in a position where freedom is lost. The perception is reinforced by bad faith (Denzin, 1984) and loss of responsibility for meaning construction, and redefines future violence as liberation from oppression. The prison metaphor is often used by other disempowered populations in various contexts, including old persons placed in nursing homes, often against their will, or in situations when their physical state demands removal from the home. In these conditions, they often describe their experience of self as being denied and controlled physically and emotionally. Under this constructed reality, being in care is replaced with being locked up in prison.

The other pole of the constructed experience in space is defining the visitation center as home:

> It's a place of opportunity . . . first of all, to see the kid without having to confront my ex-wife. . . . Every meeting outside involved emotional and financial blackmail: Z"I'll bring him to you; I won't bring him to you; you pay me; if you won't pay me, you won't see him." Every meeting involved a struggle, you never know how it will end. . . . It can end up at the police station. Just a journey into the

unknown. Today, I come here like to a real home . . . and I think that David [son's fictitious name] feels at home here too.

The contrast in the constructed spatial experience has to do with coming home, being at home. Many clients described their physical home as no home. This father describes a space where he feels safe, without being threatened by his former wife. The center is a secure, permanent locale, "a real home," as he puts it. The experience of home contrasts with the chaos and the absurd that have been forced upon him, and provides a secure corner in a non-secure world, which often creates extreme anxiety and a sense of annihilation. The professionals in this construction become parental figures who protect. The presentation of self-space is reinforced by the professional staff in statements like "you can talk about everything in this room."

Space and time

Space and time are interconnected. Améry (1994) wrote that the experience of being young as opposed to old can be understood through the differential experience of space and time. For the young, space is open and time is not limited. As people age, their experience is increasingly one of passing, consumed time, which limits the previous experience of time as open. There is a sense of growing exclusion from space associated with experiences such as facing ageism. When you age, people gradually stop asking you questions like "what would you want to do?" There is a subjective sense of gradual diminishing of options, and old persons tend to experience themselves through remembering the past. The following case example is illustrative.

A social worker received a referral from a woman who lived in a relatively remote, faraway place. She told the worker that her father lost his wife (the referring person's mother) about 6 months earlier. The daughter described several changes in her father, such as weight loss, lack of will to eat, loss of energy, and change in the relationship with the grandchildren. The daughter was concerned that he was depressive. Attempts to discuss the issues with the father failed, and he demanded that she stop relating to him as a child. The daughter asked the social worker to examine her father's situation. At the social worker's meeting with the father, he described the loss of the love of his life and his wish to die, but he expressed no intention to commit suicide. The key sentence illustrating his attitude toward life was: "What is there waiting for me? Nothing." He generalized this attitude toward the future, suggesting that the sense of having reached his boundaries was central to his human experience. Boundaries marking space and time indicate the existential experience of the void, the end of the physical world.

Others in space

Relationships are often experienced through their spatial quality. As van Deurzen-Smith (1997) pointed out, "[r]elating is, to a large extent, about space. It is regulated by the proximity of others and plays itself out as a contest over territory—gained, lost, never had or shared" (p. 117). We relate to others by the extent of closeness or distance in space, not as a measurable entity but rather as a symbolic one. Couples in crisis describe becoming distanced from each other, while living in the same house or even the same room. For example, we say "her behavior distanced her from me," or when talking about parents, "our relationships are not as close as they used to be" or "there were ups and downs in the relationship."

Boundaries are an additional dimension in relationships expressed spatially. The sense of loss of boundaries, breaking through boundaries, or lack of boundaries reflects symbolic expressions of relationships in space. Cohn (1997) noted in relation to the changing nature of relationships that their understanding was possible only through the symbolic use of space: "If existence is 'being-in-the-world', it is 'spatial'—that is, part of the wider context to which it is related. But the space between different parts of this context is not measurable in feet and yards but is experienced differently at different times; what is close today, can be distant tomorrow" (p. 14).

Similarly, being with others is expressed symbolically in spatial terms. The use of theatrical expressions is a case in point. Many clients express their experience in histrionic terms: "I feel that most of my life is a big show: I'm acting in a show, everyone is watching me, and they have no idea that it's all fake." Such self-presentation is expressive of alienation from self and others, and from everyday acts. Another symbolic form used to represent a relationship is the wall metaphor: "A wall has been erected between us." The related expression, "I need to barricade myself as self-defense," conveys the same idea.

The body in space

A central axis of being in space is the body. Merleau-Ponty (1945/2012) emphasized the duality of the body: we have a body and we are body. According to his view, our perception is not simply visual. It is primarily body-related, pre-reflective, and it constitutes the source from which all awareness and experience evolves, how we locate and make sense of the world. Merleau-Ponty distinguished between two forms of "bodiness": one related to the objective body, the body as a physiological entity, a machine functioning according to given rules; the other related to the body as awareness in which we live, and which creates us as bodily subjects. Existentially speaking, individuals in the world know themselves by their body. The body is the center of human activity by which the individual acts upon the world. This body prioritizes and interprets whatever one comes across; it is not an external cover for a soul hidden inside but rather an expression of one's existence and relation to the world. As such, the body cannot be reduced to the status of a separate object or subordinated to the mind. Existence is an activity of the lived body in intimate contact with the world. A basic human experience is feeling at home in one's body or being alienated from one's body. From this perspective, suffering from psychosomatic illness is not the result of inner or outer activities, nor is the body subordinated to emotional pressures, but rather provides its own orientation in space and in relationships with others.

The attempt to distinguish between body and soul is an illusion, as there is no clear-cut boundary between the two. As Cohen (1997) stated: "Mental and bodily aspects of experience are always involved simultaneously, though sometimes one aspect and sometimes the other aspect is accentuated" (p. 62). Consider situations in which individuals try to establish control over their eating, and in doing so, they seek to divert attention from existential concerns, as reflected in statements common to anorectic or bulimic persons: "My problems seemed out of my control, I lost my way in life. I hated the life I had, but whatever I ate and how much I weighed were under my control. Originally, I was getting compliments for my looks, but later I lost control. Fasting became a must."

The sense of belonging and ownership is a basic existential experience that determines the boundaries between the individual and the world. The body is not a given in an objective space. One can live with being disoriented in space, but subjectively individuals always listen to their body and in this way preserve the existential body. In cases of ontological insecurity, the experience is one of a harmed body, associated with a sense of loss of control and helplessness, leading to an overall threat to the sense of bodily worldliness. When existential anxiety sets in, one uses the body as means to attune to the world. The experience can be of hard or permeable boundaries, or of feelings of dissociation. These can be seen as attempts to disconnect between the body and the self, thereby disconnecting one's being from the world. Embodiment is actualized in the intersubjective world. For example, the embodiment of shame is not only personal but transmitted to the other through the body. Rape or other forms of sexual abuse are a case in point. "I'm so ashamed that I feel I'm all disgusting, desecrated, defective, damaged. I must hide, I must be alone, far from others, so no one would know who I am . . . I must shower again and again, till everything is off, to feel relief. But after a while my body is filled with disgust." And in another testimony: "I have often used the word 'void,' meaning that I feel empty, and that is something that kind of fills me up, physically and mentally . . . not that it really fills me up, neither physically nor mentally, but the urge is there, a kind of void. I was bulimic for a while, I tried to starve myself . . . I took laxative pills, drugs, not only grass you know, I tried all kinds. I didn't get so addicted but I needed to try something that would fill up that void, I don't care about limits . . . What comes to mind at this moment is a kind of panic which makes me want to grasp onto something." The "something" she was referring to was sexual relations with strange men.

These quotations from two women refer to the bodily experience in relationships with others. Because of the trauma, the space lacks the capacity to support or defend. The body adopts the view of others, of society at large, and as such reinforces the estrangement of the woman from herself; it turns against her. The personal space, emptied out or desecrated, makes its existence questionable, together with her being in the world. Yet her empty body becomes a permanent escort and source of shame and suffering. Anything used in attempts to erase this experience, including sex, drugs, and food, exacerbates her shameful body/space. Telling others is dangerous because it emphasizes her being different and worthy of shame. The body becomes the locus of experiencing the ruined personal and social identity.

The body in illness

A key feature of our existence is living the dual dialectics between illness and health. Sontag (1990) wrote that "[e]veryone who is born holds dual citizenship, in the kingdom of the well and in the kingdom of the sick. Although we all prefer to use the good passport, sooner or later each of us is obliged, at least for a spell, to identify ourselves as citizens of that other place" (p. 3). Sontag reflected on the duality of existence in spatial metaphors. Health is temporary and unreliable, and the limitations of expected illness are inevitable. But individuals are reluctant to recognize signs of illness when they appear. The following example is illustrative.

Martin, a man of 45, divorced, called to make an urgent appointment with the social worker at a health maintenance clinic. He described weakness for several months, which culminated in losing consciousness twice and having strong tachycardia at other times. Each time he overcame the symptoms and continued his everyday life without seeing his doctor. Yet he was constantly busy expecting the time when his body would betray him. Two weeks before seeing the social worker, he fainted in the street, after which he went to see a cardiologist who found severe blockages in his coronary arteries. The physician recommended heart catheterization, which Martin could not bring himself to do. Yet he was afraid to walk in public places, lacked motivation to work, and in general felt like a shadow of himself.

It has been noted that the body is the most intimate seismograph of our being. It also represents us vis-à-vis the world. Martin lost trust in his body and perceived it as his enemy, which made him vulnerable. He experienced the ambivalent feeling of the sick body as close and remote to him at the same time. The body also positions us vis-à-vis others. As such, it is dependent on us and on others at the same time. This dependence ranges from our sense of aesthetics in our perception of the body in illness by both ourselves and by others. The body enables us to be, and signals our departure from the world. It provides uniqueness, difference, and separateness together with similarity and one-ness with others. These contradictions and paradoxes become evident during illness. Martin faced losing his value in the world. His defective heart transformed his existence in the world into defective.

There is a difference in the experience of temporary, short-lived illnesses and chronic ones. During a short-lived illness (e.g., a cold, a broken limb) one has a future-focused horizon, repairing the breakdown and returning to the taken-for-granted normal state. In chronic illnesses (e.g., heart disease, cancer, multiple sclerosis), which are life-threatening and have a negative prognosis, the body becomes an obstacle to freedom, a liability, an object vis-à-vis the self and others. The body becomes transparent to others and a negative experience incorporating loss of control, freedom, choices, and empowerment. Questions such as "why me? why now?" produce doubt and insecurity in the existential space. The medical profession has no answers. Individuals are faced with the need to answer these questions by themselves, without a predefined plan or model. Such loneliness brings about deep anxiety. One experiences estrangement from the world of the healthy and a newcomer to the world of the sick. One is a deviant in one's difference, in one's departure from the normal. As a result, shame takes over as a central motif, both toward the self and others (Carel, 2016). There is increased recognition that the ability to achieve transcendence to the new situation depends on others. The body confirms the individual's need to deal with choice, responsibility, being with others, and finding meaning in suffering. As described in Chapter 2 regarding Daniel, who was suffering from multiple sclerosis, in Chapter 3 about Isaac, and in Chapter 5 about Joseph, who were both suffering from cancer, the illness was defined originally as a betrayal, and created a chaotic existence that to a great extent affected relationships with others. Intervention focused on the need for transformation and transition from a negative existential space to becoming active in creating one's world, and by doing so, achieving renewed ownership of one's being in the world. The question becomes: What kind of life is worth living with oneself and with others?

In sum, from an existential viewpoint, the space as an ontological dimension is both concrete and symbolic, and always present. Thus, existential therapy always needs to address space and the body in space, as an indispensable component of being in the world.

Existence in a nutshell

To summarize the existential approach, we stand for:

1) Existence is experienced in the dialectics between everyday life events and situations, and such basic existential themes as the absurd, suffering, insecurity, freedom, and death. There is always tension and there are gaps between these basic existential concerns and life situations. These dialectics affect our existence on the personal, interpersonal, social, and cultural levels. People experience the tension knowingly or unknowingly, and individuals experience a need to find ways of bridging between them. We act mostly at the level of life events, but the basic concerns underlie our actions.

2) An additional dialectic characteristic of our being is the tension between facticity and the freedom to act and create ourselves. Facticity is the frame within which we construct and empower ourselves. The freedom is at the same time liberating, burdensome, and confining.

3) Anxiety is a key component in the complex dialectics between gaps and bridging. This is the result of an actual or potential threat and the crisis arising from the need to find answers to deal with the basic concerns of concrete life situations, and bridge between facticity and freedom.

4) The anxiety is conducive to attempts to close the gap by choosing, acting, being committed, and assuming responsibility for the actions taken. Any action can lead either to an experience of inability to close the gap, powerlessness, and helplessness, or to an experience of responsiveness and faith in the self in the short and the long term.

5) The gaps and anxiety mentioned previously call for an effort to create and recreate the self through meaning assigned to basic questions such as: Why exist? How to be? How to interpret one's being? This may result in creating a solid ontological basis for dealing with the gap, or an experience of widening the gap, leading to ontological insecurity.

6) An important existential dimension has to do with the experience of the self with others in a social context. This dimension is also dual: others can be partners in meaning making and helpful in closing the gap and lowering anxiety, or they can be judgmental of the meaning suggested and consequently increase the anxiety experienced.

7) Throughout the existential struggle, there is conflict related to the subjectivity and uniqueness of the self in the world: on the one hand, a quest for authenticity, and on the other, a desire to erase it and in this way avoid the conflict involved in bridging efforts. Authenticity makes choice possible, ascribes meaning to action, and grants freedom. At the same time, it exacerbates conflict with others and increases the anxiety surrounding responsibility and choice.

The experience of being occurs in the context of time, particularly at the end of life. There is a time limitation to the ability to project one's self into the future. The alternative is to fail to make such a projection, to be lost in time, and experience spiraling anxiety.

7 Intervention in existential social work

The vision of existential intervention is to empower individuals to become aware of their being in the world as subjects creating meaning, choosing, acting, and taking responsibility for changing their personal and social space. Saint-Exupéry's metaphoric writing best captures our view of existential social work: "If you want to build a ship, don't drum up people to collect wood and don't assign them tasks and work but rather teach them to long for the endless immensity of the sea" (Antoine de Saint-Exupéry). Existential intervention is a way to provide vision and meaning, together with the courage to face and cope with unpredictability, lack of knowledge, and the anxiety resulting from dealing with the tumultuous sea called life.

The ideal of existential intervention is based on the following six aims: (a) living with anxiety; (b) empowering through freedom; (c) becoming responsible for choices and actions; (d) existing through ongoing meaning making; (e) being authentic toward the self and others; and (f) projecting one's being toward the future. These aims can change and co-occur, and their order is arbitrary. The best way to perceive them is through an interchangeable figure-ground perspective. They can be used in real-life situations for heuristic purposes only. The model is ideal, and as such its importance lies in understanding the dynamics of change generated with respect to each goal and to all of them in interaction. Such a way of living cannot be total, but we should aim for a sufficiently good existential orientation in our intervention.

Living with anxiety

Existential intervention is aimed at enhancing awareness about how anxiety is born, evolves, and affects one's life. It seeks to develop a secure base in individuals by enhancing their ability to confront anxiety in the midst of personal, interpersonal, and social chaos. The expected outcome of such intervention is the development of a courageous attitude toward the ultimate concerns caused by life challenges, dilemmas, conflicts, paradoxes, freedom, and choices (Deurzen & Adams,

DOI: 10.4324/9781003322085-8

2011). Yalom emphasized the need to address anxiety resulting from the ultimate concerns of death, freedom, isolation, and meaninglessness. The first step on this road involves the ability to openly elaborate and detail the anxiety arising from the lived experience, or what Spinelli termed "currently-lived world view" (Spinelli, 2007, p. 86). In the course of intervention, when clients share their everyday experiences, there is increasing emphasis on directly addressing the basic issues such as death, meaninglessness, and freedom. This goes along with an increased experience of the absurd concerning the *why* and the *what* of existence. Clients usually bring to professional encounters acute basic issues of meaninglessness, foreignness, and alienated existence, together with the resulting overall anxiety. In the course of the intervention, clients develop increased readiness to face and externalize the emotions associated with the basic issues and the related absurdity. They are increasingly capable of using these ontological concepts heuristically to describe their experience. On the ontic level, such a process enables them to contain and lower their anxiety by making informed choices and gaining a sense of participation, control, and direction in their life. Beyond that, the individual can connect between the everyday-ontic and the generalized ontological forms, and by doing so, formulate a worldview that goes beyond a given situation.

Empowering through freedom

Two parameters define the extent of success or failure of this aim. First, we must reject the idea that we are victims of external powers and abandon the belief that we are doomed to lack of freedom, and that something or someone outside ourselves can free us (May, 1958). Success is tested against the extent to which we are absolved from a rigid lifestyle, blocking the attitude and experience of freedom (Spinelli, 2007). Second, we must acquire a sense of dialectics between facticity and freedom (Sartre, 1943/1966). Neither facticity nor freedom is an exclusive factor determining the experience of being in the world. The expected outcome is that under any condition, however victimizing or intrusive circumstances may be, we still experience ourselves as free to choose and actualize decisions. van Deurzen-Smith (1997) suggested to "strive to help clients to rediscover the nature of their particular characteristics and limitations to make the most of them and turn them to good use" (p. 236). The expected outcome of this process is the realization that additional possibilities are available, which exercise greater control over our lives than we thought they do. In this way, our chances to overcome the excuses and justifications arising from attempts to deal with anxiety increase. In parallel, our capacity to integrate contradictions, paradoxes, and seemingly mutually exclusive versions is enhanced. Spinelli (2019) summarized this by stating that "truthfulness may not set us free but is likely to imbue us with the courage to face our ways of being *as we live them* rather than as we might prefer, expect, demand and/or fear living them" (p. 74).

Being responsible for choices and actions

Existential intervention aims to help individuals realize the choices and possibilities they themselves have created as active subjects of freedom (Schneider, 2007; Thompson, 1992). Two dimensions can be identified to achieve this goal. First, the recognition that we cannot escape suffering and cannot escape freedom in actualizing difficult choices. We become aware that every choice stems from a range of possible choices, and we have no way of knowing for sure what the consequences of any given choice are. This includes the understanding that choosing one option over another is associated with ontological guilt, regret, and anguish over missing opportunities and making the wrong choices. The change is envisioned in the individual's reorientation toward moral personal responsibility for doing, without projecting blame or responsibility onto others or onto circumstances (Yalom, 1980; Spinelli, 2007). The second concerns the obligation arising from dilemmas, suffering, challenges, and crises associated with being in the world. How can life situations involving inherent anxiety be transformed into empowerment arising from anxiety's creative potential? The main challenge facing individuals in handling difficult situations is to view themselves capable of transcending the natural tendency of dealing with a difficulty by evading the situation. The preferred attitude is to perceive life situations as an ontological opportunity to choose and take responsibility.

Existing through meaning making

Individuals construct stories of their lives mirroring the way in which they make sense of the world and account for their experience within the framework of values and beliefs acquired and taken for granted. Clients often feel discouraged and powerless when it comes to giving their subjectivity a chance. Others have limited resources to construct such life stories or feel that they have little to tell. For Spinelli (1997), existential intervention is "the act of revealing and reassessing the life-stories that clients tell themselves in order to establish or maintain meaning in their lives" (p. 1). To achieve meaning construction, the primary goal is to bring to life the centrality of the subjective experience of being in the world. Such subjectivity constitutes the basis for recognizing the uniqueness of the individual experience in creating meaning. The measure of success arises from the individuals' realization that meaning is an act of interpretation and they themselves are the creators of meaning, not a passive receptacle of external meaning imposed on them. Individuals are inclined to answer two questions; one is related to the importance of the story (situation, life event); the second is about the reason that accounts for its importance. Meaning is expressed in answering the big questions of life by acting.

An additional goal of existential intervention is to assist individuals in acquiring skills and habits of mind by which they can recognize wrongful assessments and self-deception regarding the meaning or the lack thereof (van Deurzen, 1997). Meaninglessness is an untenable situation; therefore, individuals search to change it in their everyday life. Individuals act from the premise that life difficulties and associated anxiety are not proof of lack of meaning but rather a challenge to construct meaningful processes in an ongoing quest for purpose (Wong, 2012).

Meaning making is the ability to reflect and account in detail for the meaning of choices and subsequent acts, in particular when defining individual uniqueness within the given limitations. Questions like: Who am I? What do I believe? What makes life worth living? How shall I live? become key for the roadmap of existence. The answers to such questions construct a coherent narrative that is presented as a "life project" (Sartre, 1943/1966). The expected outcome is that such life projects create a proactive way of being and assist in the construction of long-range goals that give life direction, control, and agency (May, 1983).

Being authentic toward the self and others

Existential intervention aims to integrate the ability to know and express one's individuality with intentionality toward relatedness and the co-creation of meaningful encounters (Spinelli, 2019). The goal is to enable individuals to relate to themselves and to others as subjects. This goal is approached from two directions. One is the development of the reflective ability of the individual concerning gaps and conflicts in relations with others. This process involves becoming conscious of the negative ways in which the self coexists with others, including insecurity, distress, anxiety, shame, loneliness, and even renunciation of the self. If successful, individuals are able to identify the many ways in which they act not authentically under the power of the "they." Throughout this process, individuals' success is signaled by their renunciation of harmful thoughts and actions. This process clarifies the active opposition to conformity and stigma-based pressures that threaten to strangle authenticity. If successful, the individuals experience liberation from an inauthentic routine in their everyday life (Krill, 1996). A key measure of success is the development of the ability to take responsibility for acts performed in "their" presence.

The second direction has to do with the process in which the individual chooses ways of self-definition as a meaning-searching subject. Choosing emphasizes the individual's ability to experience selfhood and meaning rather than avenues to provide accounts to others. This enhances moral responsibility toward others stemming from understanding the implication of one's acts on others (Levinas, 1947/1987). The measure of change is the decrease in anxiety toward others, together with the increase in the will to be responsive to them. In this way, a double aim is achieved: one is expressing the dialectics between the ontological otherness of the self and the second is related to the otherness of other protagonists in the interaction. Success is experienced if the individual achieves authenticity. The experience is one of an increased level of clarity about the interconnectedness between the individual's authenticity and the ideals, values, and actions of others.

Projecting one's being toward the future

The aim is to enable the individual to develop immediate awareness of the here and now as an opportunity to transcend it toward future meaning (May & Yalom, 1995; Yalom & Josselson, 2011). If successful, the individual willingly renounces the deterministic character and anguish of the past (Sartre, 1943/1966), for choosing a renewed commitment and responsibility to the future. In this way, the sense of orientation, control in time, and timing make possible the reconstruction of the self with renewed meaning. The individual emphasizes the freedom found in the renewed coping with being in the world as expressed in future-oriented questions, such as "What do I want from myself?" and "What do I expect to happen?" The answers enable existential autonomy. The choice is made not from a position of predicting and knowing the future, but rather from one of answering the question of the essential meaning of the present-toward-the-future. One chooses the best one can from the perspective of accepting anxiety, freedom, and choice involving meaning making within a framework of authenticity, and responsiveness toward others. This brings us back to Antoine de Saint-Exupéry's advice: "If you want to build a ship, don't drum up people to collect wood and don't assign them tasks and work but rather teach them to long for the endless immensity of the sea."

8 Toward an integrative implementation model

Existential intervention can be structured into a three-phase process, a structure well accepted in the intervention literature (e.g., Hill, 2004; Egan & Reese, 2019), as well as in existential intervention models (Spinelli, 2007). As we work through the three phases of the model, we emphasize the common elements with intervention models outside the existential tradition, and the ingredients that are unique to existential thinking.

Phase 1

Hill (2004) referred to phase 1 as exploration. During this phase, "helpers seek to establish rapport with clients, develop a therapeutic relationship, encourage clients to tell their stories, help them explore their thoughts and feelings, facilitate the arousal of emotions, and learn overall about their clients" (p. 28). Exploration under the guidance of professionals enables individuals to experience a safe space of self-reflection on the difficulties and hardships of life, as well as expectations from the therapeutic relationship. Egan and Reese (2019) assigned three tasks to this phase: "help clients (a) tell their stories, (b) reframe their stories and develop new, more useful perspectives, and begin thinking about changed, more constructive ways of acting, and (c) stay focused on the key issues and concerns that will make a difference in their lives" (p. 270). Common among the various models is the recognition of the difficulties encountered by clients in telling their story about the difficulties and challenges of life in their fullness, with authenticity and honesty, trusting an unknown other. A variety of techniques have been suggested to achieve active listening, including joint reflection on content (e.g., open questioning, summarizing, paraphrasing) and reflection on feelings (e.g., encouraging elaboration of emotions, responsive empathy, immediacy). Throughout the process, a double aim is being sought: relationships and practical implications. Relationships are enhanced by the development of trust and safety, mutuality, joint effort, and joint identification of key themes underlying and accompanying the

DOI: 10.4324/9781003322085-9

professional relationship. The second aim is to reach an agreement on the aims of therapy, to formulate joint tasks, and to clarify the changes necessary for a successful outcome. The concept of "therapeutic alliance" or "working alliance" is the actualization of this quality (e.g., Cooper, 2008; Martin et al., 2000).

Egan and Reese (2019) emphasized the need to identify "unused opportunities" in an attempt to redefine every problem as an opportunity, see the past as learning, and prepare to act toward the future, which is loaded with possibilities. One suggestion for realizing the unused opportunities, resources, and strengths comes from the strength perspective (Saleebey, 2006). Saleeby poses a series of related questions aimed at stimulating a reflection guided by eight life aspects: (a) survival questions (e.g., How did you succeed to survive despite the difficult problems you are presenting?); (b) support questions (e.g., Who are the people who supported, understood, and guided you throughout the difficult times?; (c) possibilities (e.g., How would you want your life to look?); (d) the exceptional (e.g., What changes in your behavior, thinking, and relationships when things go well for you?); (e) evaluation (e.g., What are the things you and others like about you?); (f) perspective (e.g., How do you see the contribution of the problem to your life?). (g) change (e.g., How do you think the present situation can change to your advantage?) (h) meaning (e.g., What are the most important values in your life?). The overall goal is to bring clients to adopt a proactive position vis-à-vis their problems. This includes the assumption that problems are solvable and that the self presents as a self-challenger. It also presupposes the ability to focus on issues that are workable, chose directions, tasks, and activities stemming from the understanding of the patients' life story, and the ability to develop alternative narratives concerning their life and their problems.

Existential therapy builds on these principles and embodies them to develop a specific way of thinking about intervention. The uniqueness of this first phase of existential intervention lies in helping clients explore their awareness of being in the world. May defined this as follows: "World is the structure of meaningful relationships in which a person exists and in the design of which he participates" (May, 1983, pp. 122–123). The experience of being in the world is the result of the ontological experience of the individual in the present, particularly in relation to the difficulties and decisions to be made in facing life (Yalom, 2002). Talking about the phases of existential therapy, Adams (2016) said that its aims are "to introduce, or re-introduce, the clients to the reality that they have an active part in their learning" (p. 60).

In this phase of the intervention, two dialectical dimensions must be considered. One parallels the unveiling of problems in the first phase, in which the social worker reinforces self-reflection aimed at revealing existential concerns and pressures. This can be achieved by: (a) guiding clients to examine the multiple ways in which beliefs, values, and perceptions affect decisions, actions, and feelings; (b) helping clients perceive the limitations inherent in freedom and responsibility; (c) addressing suffering and absurdity; (d) developing awareness of the ways in which the past is interpreted and how it affects the thinking and emotional processes of the clients; (e) focusing on the existential anxieties surrounding decisions and on defensive ways of dealing with them; (f) identifying and developing an understanding of mistakes and missed opportunities; and (g) living with others and being aware of the ways in which authenticity is blocked or expressed.

These issues can be actualized in several ways: (a) careful listening to the client's formulations and attempting to understand what they reflect existentially; (b) reflecting feelings and thoughts that express existential issues with regard to the client's being in the world; (c) direct questions related to existential topics. For example, in relation to death, one may ask: "If you were to die now, what would be the biggest thing you'd miss in your life?" Concerning meaninglessness, one could ask: "What are the occasions when you feel that life is not worth living?" In the area of relationships with others, it would be possible to ask: "What is the main difficulty you have in relationships with others?" The overall aim of this dimension is the attempt to develop an attitude that embraces anxiety arising from basic existential concerns as a way of understanding what is meaningful in life. The social worker is looking for overt and covert clues about things and experiences that are unique to the individual's meaning attributed to the behaviors, relationships with others, values, and worldviews.

Efforts to ascribe meaning are often hidden, paradoxical, contradictory, and at times hostile. The unveiling process is often difficult and cannot be taken for granted. The social worker acts to achieve a basic understanding of the client's fundamental project (Sartre, 1943/1966), with the aim of understanding the wholeness of the client's existence in the world. This is accomplished by the constant comparison of actions, thoughts, and emotions in various situations, based on the assumption that these represent the choices of the individual. Such understanding is merely a part of a process of intersubjective meaning making. May summarized it as follows (1983):

> The central task and responsibility of the therapist is to seek to understand the patient as a being and as being in his world. All technical problems are subordinate to this understanding. Without this understanding, technical facility is at best irrelevant, at worst a method of "structuralizing the neurosis." With it, the groundwork is laid for the therapist's being able to help the patient recognize and experience his own existence, and this is the central process of therapy.
>
> (pp. 151–152)

We must remember that the construction of the narrative surrounding the client's being in the world cannot exist in a vacuum and needs a committed audience, asking questions and acting to develop the narrative. This process of intervention is affected all along by the social worker's empathy and ability to examine the world through the client's eyes, creating for the client the experience of being understood without reservations (Yalom, 2002).

In their encounter with the clients, social workers challenge the clients to transform being in the world into a storyline with inner logic and coherence. The way clients experience their social worker is described by Spinelli (2007): "*an other who does not immediately set out to transform, reject, dispute, diminish or broadly overwhelm my worldview so that it better fits that other's worldview*" (p. 105).

People come into professional relationships with social workers in two kinds of situations: when their narrative lost significant segments that enabled safe existence, even if illusional (the loss can be immediate, chronic, or both); and when the clients are involved in conflictual situations with others, claiming that their narrative is socially unacceptable. In both situations, the social worker must ask the question "Why now?" and identify why the existing construct does not hold.

The aim of intervention is to help individuals construct the need for renewed meaning in a manner that enables a sense of hope to face the hardships of life and develop direction, achieving a sense of control. This is wonderfully expressed by the following excerpt from Alice in Wonderland:

Alice:	Would you tell me, please, which way I ought to go from here?
The Cheshire Cat:	That depends a good deal on where you want to get to.
Alice:	I don't much care where.
The Cheshire Cat:	Then it doesn't much matter which way you go.
Alice:	. . . So long as I get somewhere.
The Cheshire Cat:	Oh, you're sure to do that, if only you walk long enough.

(Lewis Carroll, *Alice in Wonderland*)

The underlying idea is that the worker and the client agreed on the meaning in the client's world and what they want to achieve in their relationship. Once this is done, they can together move to the next phase in the process.

Phase 2

Hill referred to phase 2 as insight in which "helpers collaborate with clients to achieve new understandings about clients' inner dynamics and attain new awareness of their role in perpetuating their own problems. Insight is important because it helps clients see things in a new light and enables them to take appropriate responsibility and control" (p. 30). Egan and Reese (2019) added one more layer in phase 2, which aims to help clients design the kind of change (outcome) they need or want, to set realistic goals for problem management, with the objective to discover possibilities for a better future and to develop a sense of direction and commitment to change. This working-through phase requires active involvement and responsibility of both client and social worker in enhancing awareness, self-understanding, and interpretations, while choosing specific goals for change.

Spinelli (2007) described the second phase in existential language, saying that: "What distinguishes Phase 1 from Phase 2 is that while during the former these qualities served to allow the existential psychotherapist to be 'the other' who sought to attune him- or herself to the client's presenting worldview, in Phase 2 the therapist's attempts to 'stand beside' the client is primarily expressed by challenges that are drawn from the *differences* in worldview that are also expressions of the therapist's 'otherness'" (p. 135). During the first phase, the aim is to understand and broaden the client's being in the world. In the second phase, the emphasis shifts to relatedness about content concerning active and intersubjective dialogue related to individual narratives as personal responses to the world and the existential anxiety produced by various life situations. The social worker and the client identify the multiple ways in which narratives create meaning and reinforce coping strategies, while at the same time continually identifying the basic themes that are responsible for anxiety and chaos. Practically, intervention in the second phase is a dialectic process between (a) development and reinforcement of new meanings and (b) challenging and confronting the client with regard to contradictions, conflicts, passivity, and even sabotage in the ways of constructing new meanings.

Adams (2016) summarized this phase in the intervention process:

> We will be challenging and interpreting, which means that we will be making descriptive interpretations, we will be searching with our client for accurate re-descriptions of the client's experience that help them to understand it, its context and meaning in a new way. Quite often it will mean focusing on ambiguity and referring to the paradoxes in the client's life, or how they repeat past patterns in different parts of their life.
>
> (p. 66)

Reconstructing meaning serves as a compass in setting goals and making choices concerning future acts. The social worker and the client together further examine the efforts they attempted, and which stopped or failed to create meaning. Thinking about meaning is based on the duality principle "that all negative conditions contain seeds for personal growth and all positive conditions contain hidden dangers" (Wong, 2010, p. 90).

In this process, the individual must deal with the fact that meaning is not pre-given and it cannot be found based on existing schemes or menus. It is therefore the responsibility of the individual to create it. The process described here is anxiety-producing both for the individual and the social worker. The latter copes with anxiety by discovering that meaning cannot be imported from others, and it is not a technical gimmick. Being in an active position concerning meaning making confronts the parties with the anxiety arising from multiple possible meanings and the realization that they should not cave in to anxiety arising from the freedom to choose (Hill, 2018).

Throughout the second phase, the social worker guides the dialogue concerning meaning, while striving for authenticity. On the personal level, the social worker directs to choices of meanings based on the individual freedom of a person who is unique in the world and creates and recreates oneself based on conscious choices. The social worker acts to advance meanings in the present stemming from examinations of possibilities unaffected by unwanted meanings dictated by others or conforming to normative expectations. Considering meaning from a position of the authentic inner truth is a good point of departure for the process of examining one's relations to others. In this context, social workers and their clients examine the meaning of choices and actions as part and parcel of ethics in relation to others. The result are two foci of authenticity in which one is committed to one's inner truth, and the second is connected to others in a manner that allows meaning to be tied to reality.

Encouraging the individual to experience meaning does not necessarily occur through big questions but rather through focus on life domains that give meaning in the present. Thus, the question "How shall I live?" is examined through the more concrete question "Which activity do I want to perform today?" The understanding of the social worker in this first phase concerns the belief systems, significant others, goals, and aspirations in life domains, such as work, all of which produce a stock of specific meanings for the individual. Such stock constitutes the basis for the second stage in which the individual can rely on what has been constructed in stage 1, particularly in situations where meaning is absent. Yalom (1980) pointed out that individuals need help to experience freedom, authenticity, and responsibility rather than prescriptive philosophical statements regarding these issues. This is actualized in situations where the individual is required to make decisions (Maddi, 2012; Yalom, 2002). In this second phase, the social worker encourages clients to examine potential meanings for the future toward which they tend. This can be in response to a direct question ("What do you want?"), or it may be accomplished through guided fantasy techniques or miracle questions from the solution-focused approach ("Let's fantasize that you went to sleep and all problems disappeared without your knowledge. What would be the first thing indicating that a miracle occurred and your problem went away?"). The meta-aim of the social worker is to revitalize the wish of the client as a source of hope. The choice of technique seems to be second to the ability to frame the technique used within an existential frame of reference (May, 1983). The key message to clients is that decisions made with a future orientation are potentially useful for change, whereas decisions with a past orientation focusing on loss of opportunities perpetuate their situation. The social worker acts to enhance self-compassion concerning mistaken decisions and choices, and emphasizes future meanings embodied in hopes and aspirations.

The existential confrontation is an additional dimension of the second phase

The social worker acts in the first dimension by encouraging, supporting, and guiding clients to bring to light the strength of something unique, which reaches beyond the difficulties and suffering. The social worker encourages meaning despite difficult internal and external conditions, including the negative reactions of others and social-cultural forces acting against the authenticity and positive view of the individual. The social worker challenges the client to move from search for cause or rationale, which accounts objectively for things and the ways they occur, to a position of subjectivity lacking "truth" or a unique explanation. Such dynamics are likely to increase anxiety; therefore, the social worker must confront it by preventing the client from giving in to anxiety. The question May (1958) asked was: What is the obstacle preventing clients from committing themselves unconditionally? The answer to this question helps the social worker understand the anxieties and obstacles before the clients' being in the world, which stops them from creating meaning. The existential position (Camus, 1942/1955) is that life is to be committed to without denying its absurdity. To accomplish this, the social worker must start by making clients face the lack of authenticity in their way of life, and suggest that this is conducive to illusion and suffering. This is intended to confront the sense of limitation of the individual, which is nurtured by anxiety concerning the possibilities of creating meaning. The road to not suffering goes through more suffering, and the road to meaning goes through meaninglessness.

Another component of the confrontation is related to the emphasis on human capacity for choice (Schneider, 2007). Such capacity is a critical force in the process of meaning making, but it creates further anxiety and brings about a temptation to evade choice. The social worker involved in existential confrontation points to Sartre's dictum that the individual is condemned to choose. The attention of the client is focused on the fact that in every decision there is both potential for meaning and burden accompanied by anguish. The social worker tries to convey to the client a double message: one of normalizing this anguish; the other that existential intervention does not aim to provide a pleasant evasion of reality but rather serves to remind the client that there is a need to cope with the anxiety and anguish arising from the client's life situation. Throughout this confrontation, the worker empathically encourages clients to face the contradictions and gaps in their perception of the situation, beliefs, wishes, emotions, decisions, and behaviors. If clients get off the track, the social worker is expected to refocus them assertively, yet sensitively. The confrontation is clarified by questions such as "What is it that you want?" "What do you feel?" "How will your actions make your life positive?" The client's answers will guide the social worker to the issues concerning which clients attempt to deflect responsibility to others, such as the social worker or some other external force. The social worker points out the ways in which individuals protect themselves from having to acknowledge anxiety by acts such as searching for power and control. Through these confrontations, the social worker guides individuals to the understanding of how they contribute to their own distress (Yalom, 2002).

Another domain of existential confrontation in this phase is related to revealing and deepening the experience of ontological guilt. The social worker is confronting the individual's self-alienation, which is blatant in the tendency to focus on mistaken or missed past decisions as ways of blocking possibilities and paths to the future. The social worker seeks to boost courage (Tillich, 1952/1966), at times, by encouraging steps to deal with fear, develop self-confidence, and inspire belief in the freedom and responsibility involved in the realization of authenticity.

The dialectics between meaning and anxiety are evident in decisions. The existential social worker identifies life events that have the potential of serving as boundary situations, where the client avoided making decisions and carrying out certain tasks. The social worker seeks to clarify for the client the ontological meaning and potential meanings inherent in the decision, focusing on the details attesting to avoidance of responsibility and authenticity. Yalom (1980) noted that the therapist needs to help individuals become aware of their meta-decisions. The therapist must help clients come to terms with the fact that beliefs concerning themselves or others are not necessarily the only ones possible. An instructive example is confronting the perception that past traumas and suffering imply that the freedom to choose was denied and therefore the individual gives in to a sense of helplessness. The social worker leads the client to the conclusion that the decision not to decide means abandoning freedom as a path to avoid anxiety and pain for the purpose of some ultimate concern. Focusing on existential anxiety means reorganizing the priorities in life, including avoidance of automatic actions. The confrontation brings to consciousness the denial and simultaneous encouragement to rebel as a precondition to actualize meaning. Kierkegaard summarized the confrontation with anxiety in his well-known saying that the road is not difficult, the difficulty is the road (Sagi, 2018). In other words, as Adams (2016) and van Deurzen and Adams (2011) noted, confronting one's existential anxiety helps acknowledge and identify one's freedom to realize new possibilities. Such confrontation, however, creates anxiety regarding the practical constraints of life situations and facing the others' expectations and pressures, the uncertainties, as well as the possibility of being wrong or failing.

Phase 3

Phase 3 is the "action stage" (Hill, 2004), in which the social worker and the clients develop goals and programs and make strategic decisions on how to act given the context of the client's life (Egan & Reese, 2019). It involves the learning and acquisition of skills, ways of thinking, and emotional reasoning. All these are functional in problem solving, evaluation of the effectiveness of various actions, the realization of goals and the enhancement of wellbeing. Throughout phase 3, the real world becomes the experiential locale where newly acquired knowledge and skills are tested. Spinelli (2007) referred to phase 3 as the "closing down of the therapy world," emphasizing the potential of "implementation on the part of the client of those possibilities of relatedness as experienced and examined within the boundaries of the therapy world extending beyond its boundaries and into his or her wider world of relations" (p. 178).

The dialectic is between "*within* the client's subjectivity" (p. 179) at one end and the "they-focus" (the inter-relatedness in the world) at the other. A key component of this dialectic lies in "the client's experience of how those who make up his or her wider world of others' . . . experience their own inter-relational realms in response to the client's way of relating to them" (p. 180). Throughout this dialectic process, a series of complexities emerge, some of which are conflictual and paradoxical. For example, the meaning attributed by clients does not necessarily overlap with the meanings of others. In the transition between the potential and its realization, between subjectivity and interrelatedness, the individuals may encounter the limitations on their freedom, choices, and decisions. This may lead to an experience of loss and added anxiety concerning the things they learned and understood through the therapeutic process. Thus, the individuals may try to avoid changing basic beliefs and behaviors.

The third stage in existential therapy focuses on helping clients implement what they learned and contain the anxiety in a manner that would not stop them from acting. The social worker's message is that the actualization of choices and acts depends to a great extent on what individuals want to be and in what areas they wish to grow. In this way, small decisions may become expressions of existential presence and authenticity in the world (Jaspers, 1967). According to Adams (2016), phase 3 is based on risks taken by the client. Therefore, the therapist's role is "to try to consolidate the changes made so they can be integrated into the client's idea of who they are and how they came to be. This often means pointing out how they have actually done things differently, more competently and more courageously than before" (p. 67).

During this phase, the key obstacle that needs to be addressed is the clients' possible paralysis resulting from their inability to handle uncertainty (Yalom & Josselson, 2011) and from the temptation to embrace bad faith. In coping with such experiences, clients face two extreme choices: experience the world in a manner that assumes that nothing will make any difference or believe that every action is meaningful. By encouraging clients, the social worker heightens their courage and hardens their resilience, committing them to the struggle to actualize their belief that they can usually influence the course of events. The social worker seeks to put clients into a frame of mind where they can grow and derive wisdom from positive and negative experiences (Wong, 2012). From a strength perspective, the social worker acts based on the assumption that within all individuals there are resources that enable them to cope with life and build it. Individuals may have acted out of strength in the past and in the present, and it is possible that they did not fully use their strengths or did not aim their actions in the proper direction. They should be made aware that the strength is present in them and needs to be brought to the surface (Saleebey, 2009).

In this phase, the social worker continues to reiterate that decision-making is unavoidable in everyday activity and that it constitutes the richest resource for existential experiences. The social worker focuses the client on the doing as the key potential for future meaning. Yalom (2002) emphasized the regrets individuals have on things done or not done in the past, opportunities missed, compromises made, and so on. The past is not changeable, and it can be an obstacle to the future. Yalom asked concerning the future: "What would you say if we are to meet in a year from now, what new regrets you accumulated?" His message for the future is that our key mission is to help avoid regrets. Decisions take place within a speculative context. At the same time, they need to be made by clients, in accordance with their own truth, while recognizing the consequences of the decision for others. One must recognize that there will always be a gap between one's subjectivity and one's interrelatedness.

An additional concern in the third phase is how to unify acts into an integrative vision, what Sartre termed "the fundamental project"

(Sartre, 1943/1966). This constitutes the unifying narrative for assessing the occurrences, feelings, and thoughts of the client. May (1958/1983) emphasized the will as the center of existence. The way individuals perceive their life depends in large measure on what they do with this perception. This intentionality gives meaning to being in the world. Individuals cannot know the truth before they take a position concerning their fundamental project.

Change

A distinction should be made between coping and growth. Coping helps a person to handle immediate situations, to resist stressors, and recover and survive in the position one finds himself in, which would enable maintaining continuity or returning to the previous level of functioning. Growth helps the individual to reflect on the meaning of what is being survived. This ties into Spinelli (1997)'s statement concerning intervention as quoted previously: change is awareness of the client's revelation and reassessment of "life stories that clients tell themselves in order to establish or maintain meaning in their lives" (p. 1). Our criteria for change are related to the individuals' awareness of the stories they narrate to themselves, reflect over their intensity, losses, and gains, perceive these narratives as their own choices and develop the ability to create alternative stories.

The expected outcome is that by changing, clients become capable of creating their own unique fundamental project, enabling them to be in the world, despite the complexities of the givens, in a more authentic way and connected to the world of others. Spinelli (2016) pointed to the fact that experiencing change is a challenge to security, constancy, and continuity. The extent of change can be assessed based on the ability of the narratives to reflect the experience of in-between change and continuity and at the same time embrace their polarities. The essential change arises from destabilizing or restructuring one's own worldview, and our ability to "embrace its unknown possibilities and consequences" (p. 135). The change lies in the continuity we experience despite the anxiety arising from concrete and symbolic losses. This is particularly evident when examining choices involving the denial of alternatives (Yalom, 2002). Spinelli (2016) noted that the symbolic meaning of accepting change is an experience of "movement towards death." According to him, "the reflective acceptance of a change event signals the 'death' of the currently maintained worldview" (p. 136). We seek to evaluate the outcome of our intervention based on the extent to which it succeeded in the attempt to reconfigure one's being in the world more authentically. Here we use Calhoun and Tedeschi's (1999) conceptualization of post-traumatic growth, who identified three dimensions of change: changed philosophy of life; change in the sense of self: vulnerable but stronger; and changed sense of relationships with others.

A changed philosophy of life involves a switch in the individual's world-view concerning the meaning of failure, pain, and suffering. Such change involves a transformation of painful life events, enabling the individual to reevaluate the meaning of life, change priorities, and develop a philosophy before death, based on the spiritual approach. This transformed worldview makes possible sufficient liberation from the experience of endangered existence. Life becomes a valuable commodity motivated by ongoing search for meaning.

Changed sense of self: Vulnerable but stronger

Whereas the first dimension is aimed at developing a passion for meaning, the second is directed toward changing the individual's self-perception from a passive to an active one. Individuals recognize the vulnerabilities imposed by life, but instead of perceiving themselves as victimized, their tendency is to focus on their unique capacities. Through such changes, they come to value their strengths and develop additional ones, which enable them to identify and develop new meanings. Wong (2012) pointed out that one of the indications of impending change is that "in place of debilitating anxiety or depression there is emotional and behavioral vitality" (p. 76). To the same dimension of change of self, we can attribute what van Deurzen-Smith (1997) called "accepting limitations." "This can only come about from coming to terms with our inner facticity in the shape of our physical and personal characteristics, which are inherited genetically and which form part of the givens that we have to work within this world. Accepting our heritage does not amount to being fatalistic" (p. 236). She went on to explain what it means to come to terms with lack: "To make the most of our sense that something is always missing is to allow ourselves to go out of ourselves in order to seek to be fulfilled" (p. 237). This reflects the interplay between vulnerability and strength in existential thought.

Changed sense of being with others

This dimension expresses change in empowering sensitivity toward others, increased closeness to significant others, and sensitivity to human suffering. The change is expressed in the ability to communicate openly about feelings directed at others from a position of increased empathy and compassion. Such change is evident in the recognition of the separate subjectivity of each individual, in the assumption of personal responsibility within the intersubjective relationship (Wong, 2012).

Termination of the professional relationship: Finality
with no end

As described by Spinelli (2007), the end must be examined in light of the question: "*What is it about a particular ending that permits or prevents me from embracing it as appropriate to this particular relationship?*" (p. 189). This connects with what Iacovou and Weixel-Dixon (2015) asked: "What, then, are the signals that designate an appropriate timing or an ending? This query infers that there is a 'true' or 'valid' reason for making a choice, or more specifically, the 'right' choice" (p. 132). It is not easy to answer these questions because in many ways the end is related to the entire narrative of the intervention process, and in some other ways it has a life of its own. Most of the time, the end is the beginning of a new narrative, and as such a bridge to the future. No ending can be seen as final, and many seemingly contrasting elements are part of it. Adams (2016) wrote that

> a good ending does not mean that all loose ends have been tied up and everything is understood. This is the end of learning and is a delusion. It means that both the therapist and the client have confidence that the client has learnt enough about self-reflection and a philosophical understanding of living to be equal to any further "slings and arrows of outrageous fortune" that may come their way.
>
> (p. 86)

All we can hope for is that a good ending leaves the client knowledgeable and yearning for developing a new narrative of life, and in possession of the strength to deal with it.

Case illustration

The following case illustrates the existential intervention process.

Adam is 40, divorced for 10 years, father of two adolescent boys who live with their mother. He works as a tour guide. He attended university for several years but never finished his studies. He has no academic degree or profession, his work is seasonal, and he has no occupational security. He loves his work, derives great satisfaction from it, but he feels that the insecure income is a burden. After he pays the child support, he has a modest income left over for himself. Overall, Adam makes the impression of a man with a good sense of humor who enjoys life. And yet, he perceives himself as defective and feels that he has not much to offer to a potential partner without a solid financial base, without a profession, and with fragile health due to his diabetes. Adam has been treated at a diabetic clinic for years, where the staff seems frustrated with him: on the one hand, he seems intelligent and elicits positive feelings in those around him; on the other hand, his behavior is self-destructive. Because of his severe diabetes, he must inject insulin several times a day, and must test his sugar level to establish the right dosage. Adam neglects to perform these tests and maintains that they are painful. As a result, he injects himself blindly, without adjusting the dose to the level of his sugar, often experiencing hypoglycemia, when he can eat sweets to his liking. He is suffering from severe obesity. Moreover, his inappropriate treatment results in unbalanced sugar, which creates a series of health problems. One is the deterioration of his vision, which is irreversible, although it could be stopped with proper management of the diabetes. Second, he has kidney problems, which would require a series of preventive steps to avoid further deterioration. The staff at the diabetes clinic feels helpless. He tends to disappear periodically from the clinic, and return sporadically for care, at his leisure. At times he feels that his behavior is out of control and is wary of meeting the staff because he does not want to confront their reactions. The social worker initially seeks to make him respond better to treatment, which the social worker considers to be a lifesaving activity.

Intervention: Phase 1

The social worker attempts to understand Adam's being in the world. Adam views himself as a spontaneous person; therefore, he does little planning and goes with the flow. This is manifested by the need to eat uncontrollably. He understands that he is harming himself, but all through the meetings, he presents himself as unwilling to give up his spontaneity, which he uses as a barrier against becoming a sad person who wants no part of life. He opts for an "either all or nothing" approach. His existential anguish stands in the way of seeing himself as a person who has a choice and can control his eating habits. The social worker attempts to reveal the reasons behind his anguish. How does he make decisions and why? She tries to instill in him a more positive attitude toward medical care. But Adam fails to understand. Why does he have to try? For whom? Increasingly, the therapeutic encounters reveal that Adam perceives his body as defective for himself and others, with no control over its functions and dependence on the chronic state of his illnesses. His avoidance of medical care following the prescribed protocol is meant to silence the experience of the body as hostile and to avoid the eruption of negative feelings, such as anger and jealousy. The body is experienced as the prison guard of the self in the joint space with others. It allows little space for freedom and authenticity. He experiences death anxiety every time he is hypoglycemic. He talks about death as an imminent possibility, and often mentions the fact that he will not want to live if he becomes blind or dependent. Suicide is a realistic option for him, as he thinks that life has no special meaning. He considers satisfaction and independence as conditions for living. The therapeutic conversations reveal his view of the illness as a sort of a cruel destiny that brought about his transformation from a normative child into an adult unlike others, who lost the taste for living. The gap between Adam's self-perception as an empty vessel, rotten inside and nicely packaged to give the impression that he is a pleasant person, lighthearted and good natured, revealed the gap between his social and personal self. At this point, the social worker tries to connect Adam to the ontic level. She reflects to him an individual's experience of thrownness into a destiny associated with a sense of entrapment and anxiety related to his concrete health and his interpersonal and professional situation. His sense is one of entrapment in factuality and loss of control in most areas of his life. The presence of death in his life increases the threat of failure and the sense of the absurd in his life. The result is severe paralysis in the area of choice and action. Taking responsibility for his actions is perceived as further senselessness and absurdity. The paralysis experienced by Adam reflects inability to perceive life events as challenges to meaning, and to view himself as a creator of meaning. The outcome is being-from-estrangement of the self, alienated from the continuity of time toward the future and blocked from being in an authentic life. The social worker discusses with Adam topics such as emptiness, self-description in negative terms, emphasis on failures, lack of will, and wrong decisions. This gradually enables him to express and contain the anxiety, and to understand the multiple ways in which his ontic experiences are tied to his choices responsible for failing in treatment. He comes to understand increasingly that investment in balancing his sugar is related to basic existential issues and is an expression of loss of meaning.

To counterbalance his negative experience of the world, the social worker questions Adam about the meaningful things left in his life. He describes his relationship with his children and his love for them, and the importance he attributes to these relationships. To the question of how his children perceive him he answers that his children understand that he is not healthy, they are concerned about his health, and share these concerns with him openly. The social worker explores the extent to which he is aware of the level of understanding of the children of his illness and the messages he conveys to them concerning life. In this way, the social worker mirrors Adam's ultimate concern, as it is manifest in meaninglessness, helplessness, and lack of choice, which he conveys to his children, frightening them in the process. The turning point in moving from the first phase to the second is Adam's questioning whether there is anything positive he can pass on to his children, as he attempts to deal with his illness.

Intervention: Phase 2

For Adam, his children were a key junction, and they reflect the obligation to face his belief that he is a victim of the cruel illness forced upon him. He is now asked to recognize the illness as a limitation that does not deny his freedom to choose and take a position concerning his fatherhood. Intervention focused on his power to create meaning, which helps transcend his bodily situation and overcomes the expectation that he needs to minimize his spatial presence in being. The turning point comes about as he experiences coping reframed as an opportunity to transmit to his children the principle of taking responsibility. He makes the change by participating in treatment and begins to be responsive to the medical intervention he is expected to undergo. Nevertheless, there are various regressive episodes, when Adam leaves and then returns to the program. The social worker confronts him about these episodes, which she explains as attempts to avoid anxiety and cope with the body as the author of life difficulties and their implications, for both the children and himself. During phase 2, the social worker clarifies that the hope to avoid and free himself from anxiety and anguish leads nowhere. Adam describes the body as betraying him, leading to loss of power, self-pity, inability to handle pain, and discomfort. He further reports difficulties sticking to the diet and keeping up with sports activities and abandons the diet. He attributes the roller coaster response to a lack of willpower. His self-perception is one of "either all or nothing" and "if this is hard, I give it all up." Such responses are associated with disappointment and low self-esteem. Adam reveals thoughts about suicide as an option. He casts doubt about his right to exist, saying that "I make my parents suffer, I cannot function according to their expectations, I'm sick and defective, and will likely become an invalid and a burden. I want no part of it. I am friendly and funny outward, but at the end of the day I'm alone, with no partner. I have nothing to present to anyone because I am expected to give more than I can offer. I failed in my marriage."

The social worker intervenes to clarify that there is a need to examine life's givens (ultimate concerns) and not focus on death as part of the illness. This position is exacerbated by the refusal to persevere in the treatment plan. Adam's existential isolation is aggravated by his lack of authenticity and his unwillingness to recognize that he is free to create meaning in a chaotic world. Courage is needed not to seek to avoid anxiety but act despite it. The social worker points out that Adam's attitudes and actions express avoidance to create meaning and limit his existence to symptoms. This gains expression mostly in the way he handles his body in space. He presents the defective body as limiting his powers and abilities, as they are expressed in relationships with the self and others. In this way, he avoids being in the world and avoids the question: What can I do to take a small step forward? Such questions assert the need to face the immediate future. Fear is an expression of the anxiety caused by the future in general and by the actions he is expected to take to achieve being authentic in the world. Any attempt on Adam's part to avoid taking such action reflects his tendency to avoid facing the ultimate concern related to meaninglessness, death, and isolation. The social worker seeks to convey that only facing the anxieties related to the ultimate concern will enable him to address the lack of completeness, which in turn is the way to contain anxiety. One way to do it is to realize that all control over life and body, in time and space, is partial and situational. The focus of intervention is on self-treatment of the diabetes, seeking to establish priorities, classify difficulties, and choose paths to deal with the illness from a position of understanding the anxieties created by it.

Adam's choice should be to see in the dialogue with his children an opportunity to show responsibility to cope with bad faith: to show Adam that he has a degree of freedom, contrary to his dominant self-perception as weak and powerless. The social worker tries to encourage recognition of the transcendence of his fatherhood into a narrative of heroism for the sake of the children who are exposed to his attitude. By doing so, she conveys the message that there are external circumstances, such as the illness, that do not stand in the way of freedom, choice, and authenticity toward the self and others. Adam is called upon to recognize his existential guilt for what he does and what he fails to do particularly concerning the actualization of values and the price to pay for those he fails to actualize. The social worker makes the connection between the existential guilt about the illness and the guilt for failing the treatment and missing the opportunities to succeed.

The social worker's position is that although there is no way of avoiding the sense of social isolation, Adam can experience a sense of control by increased connectedness and engagement, participation, and contribution to others. Adam is able to see his false presentation of self and develops the ability to connect. He makes new contacts that are real and open. In the process, he is able to enhance his self-acceptance despite the deficiencies he identifies in himself.

Another focus in this phase is the issue of meaning creation. At the beginning of the second phase, Adam presents himself as experiencing a loss of values and being anxious, without a stable identity. He describes himself as moving around aimlessly, with no direction or purpose. His life as he experiences it appears to be a succession of events over which he has no control. The social worker helps Adam to explore his behaviors as he searches for purpose. She examines with him the key values he adheres to, what he feels he has succeeded to achieve and where he failed. These questions bring him closer to his unique search for identity, while he recognizes his strong ties with normative expectations and conformism. His challenge now is to achieve authentic and direct self-expression.

Throughout the second phase, the social worker focuses on the present-toward-the-future. The past serves as context, but it does not limit Adam's freedom to make changes with regard to his medical condition, professional status, and relationships with significant others.

In summing up the second phase, we can identify two critical axes: one is related to the expectations of Adam to examine his blocking of anxiety, which disables his personal growth; the other is to choose and inculcate attitudes that enhance choice, freedom, and responsibility, and to organize his life according to authentic expectations.

Intervention: Phase 3

During this phase, the changed perceptions and attitudes toward existence and the individual's world are clarified and crystallized. The emphasis shifts to narrative change, which helps the move from lack of agency to self-empowerment in organizing existential abilities. The individual still holds to the themes of being in the world, but the focus is on re-interpretation. We illustrate these changes along three dimensions: transformations in the anxiety concerning the relationships to the ultimate concern; focusing on the dominant meaning as a basis for a renewed interpretation of life; and laying the foundations of authenticity and relatedness.

Transformations in anxiety take place in Adam's experience while he is coping with anxiety and the ontological insecurity arising from attempts to actualize freedom, choice, and responsibility. This is evident in Adam's attitude toward death. During the first phase, Adam emphasizes his provocations in relation to death by refusing to follow medical directions, denying his physical situation, and regarding suicide as a plausible solution. During the second phase, a confrontation takes place concerning his self-perception of lacking freedom and power in the face of death, and his attempts to control death by submission to it. The attempts to provoke death disappear in the third phase. Adam renounces bad faith, and the acceptance of death as an existential possibility is imminent. The understanding that death is a continuation of life and inseparable from it leads to responsibility, as illustrated by his attitude toward suicide. Adam reaches the understanding that suicidal preoccupation is a denial of responsibility, associated with a false illusion of freedom, with no consideration of the implications, particularly for his children. Throughout the second phase, the focus is on attempts to clarify and confront the ways in which Adam is contemplating his misery as a diabetic, with a sealed destiny, avoiding his anxiety and denying freedom and choice. In the third phase, his orientation emphasizes his will, self-value, and the power he has to withstand the illness. He recognizes that he exists and that his life is essential and meaningful despite the anxiety involved in the possibility of death. The visible expression of the change is in his commitment to follow medical guidelines and persevere in his treatment and diet. Even when he fails, he remains committed to resuming the program rather than searching for accounts that reflect bad faith. Adam's onto-logical anxiety transforms into existential guilt, as expressed in taking responsibility for his life. This is evident in an event in which a physician who related to his tests casually ended up increasing his insulin intake. Adam perceived this as an irresponsible medical decision, which brought him to the conclusion that he alone is responsible for his treatment and needs to take charge of his own care more closely.

Meaning as key to existence

In the third phase, the realization of the impossibility to change the facts and circumstances becomes evident, and there is increasing faith in the need to use freedom in order to change the relationship and adjust it to the existing context. All during the second phase, Adam is continually hurt by the belief that the illness directs his life, and as a result, his self-perception is one of sickness and human deficiency. In the third phase, Adam refocuses on transforming meaning based on the understanding of what wishes and values he needs to actualize are, and how to define himself in light of these wishes and values. All this takes place in the context of attempting to redesign a fundamental life project focusing on what is unique in his existence and on how he can actualize his strengths within this project. One of his key meaning systems revolves around his professional identity. In contrast to the first and second phases, in which he emphasizes his doubts, failures, and bad choices, in the third phase, he focuses on the value of his choice of being a tour guide, which actualizes his authentic choices. He further takes responsibility for finding a perma-nent framework that can ensure and bolster his economic stability. To substantiate his changed attitude, he submits his candidacy to work on a professional and social project, which he previously shunned because of his anxieties and illness. He succeeds in joining this project, which forces him to develop an entire system of procedures and support related to his illness, and chooses meaning without allowing the illness to impose limits on him. During this phase, Adam expresses the motif of finding coherence in his activity based on purpose, significance, and value, even as he faces chaos and meaninglessness. Adam's actions are tested and confirmed as the realization of challenges resulting from his choices. At this point, the therapeutic encounters focus on finding paths to maximize his particular qualities, hopes, and aspirations, as a basis for constructing meaning and an ongoing examination of how realistic his goals are in the face of the circumstances. The key question for him remains "What for?" not in the sense of the absurd but rather as a basis for his choices and directed actions. Meaning reconstructs his future orientation, enhances his sense of freedom and responsibility, and helps him avoid wasting resources over unnecessary conflicts, anxieties, and behaviors that are not conducive to meaningful narratives.

Laying the foundation of authenticity and relatedness

Throughout the second phase, the confrontation with Adam centers around his perception of threat from others, aiming to objectify him and thereby forcing him to falsify his self. For example, in relation to medical treatment, he perceives others (medical staff) as attempting to deny his freedom of being spontaneous and deny him the small enjoyments of life, such as eating his preferred foods. Such ideas begin to be contested during the second phase, in relation to his perception of his children. In the third phase, there is broad recognition of the need to become an individual, acknowledging personal commitment and authenticity together with the need to weigh the consequences of being for others and the implications of others on the self. Adam understands that his perceptions have limited to a great extent his freedoms to be a subject, and implicitly, helped him avoid responsibility toward others. Assessing the implications of such change with great concern, Adam is interested in feedback from the social worker. In particular, he wants the transcendentality of his actions toward his children, as a guiding principle, to be viewed as authentic. This encourages him to examine the meaning of his life in most of its domains.

During the third phase, Adam is conscious of the lack of authenticity in his behaviors and of the need to solidify authentic aims that fit the meanings he himself has created. Adam is aware of the fact that he uses the past to hold firm his relationships with the world. He is ready to relate to the professional's criticism as learning and guidance about the ways in which he can use the freedom of choice more constructively. He is seeking support and encouragement in the professional relationship to overcome the fear of mistakes from the past, which reinforced his anxiety about authenticity and relationships with others. For example, in contrast to past patterns, when Adam tended to present his professional qualifications as taken for granted and subject to cynicism and denial, in the third phase the question is how his actions can become an authentic contribution to others, and how the feedback he receives can foster his authenticity. This change has to do with Adam's choice of a social and professional project (described in the section related to meaning), which forced him to upgrade his qualifications and his abilities related to others.

During phase 3, a change takes place in his experience of failure toward his parents, who are university graduates (whereas Adam failed in his academic studies). Emphasis shifts from external focus on biography as an expression of "I'm a failure and lazy" to one of choices made. Adam examines his existence in time from a perspective of future orientation, including the recognition that some of his failures he can fix while some he cannot. Adam's question becomes "What can I do at this time within the limitations imposed by the choices made in the past, in a way that is empowering and helpful in overcoming the anxieties of ultimate concerns, while reinforcing my authentic meaning?"

In sum, for Adam, the third phase is one of placing decision-making, free will, and responsibility at the center of his experience. He comes to believe in strengthening his choices and his faith in his decisions and is cognizant of the need to act accordingly. The emerging narrative emphasizes the sense of symbolic unity of the various domains in his life (illness, children, parents, biography, profession, life circumstances, and life and death in general). All these become expressions of actualized choices, responsibility, and meaning. His ability to end the professional relationship is based on the recognition that Adam has a future life plan, a fundamental project, with well-founded recognition of his courage to struggle for a renewed narrative of his existence.

9 Relationships in existential intervention

A key axiom in existential intervention, as in most clinical interventions, is that meaningful relationships have a strong healing effect (Willis, 1994; Yalom, 2002). The starting point in relationships in existentialism, as described by Krill (1996), is a view of the client as "a unique, irreplaceable worldview that is in the process of growth, emergence, and expansion" (p. 260). This attitude toward relationships with clients in existential intervention commits the social worker to intervene from a position of consciousness concerning the clients' lived experiences and inter-subject relationships, allowing space for existential struggles and coping. Thus, relationships assume intensive empathy, presence, mutuality, and authenticity, all of which are elaborated in the present chapter. The social worker initiates the realness of the relationship by stating her responsibility in elaborating on the overall character of the intervention and its aims (Iacovou & Weixel-Dixon, 2015). Relationships do not liberate from existential isolation and struggles but help clients face and handle them.

Empathy

From Buber's standpoint, the intersubjective space amounts to "the recognition of an ontological dimension in the meeting between persons" (Friedman, 2008, p. 300). In this manner, empathy is responsiveness to the other's call, and as such, the basis of relationships. van Deurzen-Smith (1997) elaborates this empathic understanding as follows: "Existential work can only be done efficiently if the therapist is willing to be touched by the client's material. The work is based on the notion that there are universal human concerns" (p. 196). At the most basic level, the social worker is to reach out and attempt to understand the client's world. Yalom's metaphor (2002) for this attitude is "looking out the patient's window" (p. 17).

The social worker's willingness to "love" the client from a position of existential unity leads to an intersubjective space in which even opposite

DOI: 10.4324/9781003322085-10

directions do not harm the basic recognition of the other's experience. According to van Deurzen-Smith (1997), "Therapists who do not have such an ability to lend themselves to temporarily identify with the client's position, and to live into the client's preoccupation, will be hard put to work from a position of resonance. Resonance is this ability to tune into the dimension of a person's troubles and to figuratively let the vibrations of it set off a similar sound in oneself" (p. 196). This creates an expectation from the therapist "to be an other who, in the act of embracing the alien worldview of the client, seeks to permit that worldview to co-habit the therapy world without threat of its being distorted, amended, altered or rejected by the other's (i.e., the therapist's) more powerful worldview" (Spinelli, 2007, p. 109). From this perspective, empathy changes beyond anxiety, knowledge, and expectations of the other professionals involved, to what Buber conceptualized as "confirmation" (Friedman, 2002). The confirmation means that beyond accepting the other, there is empathy toward the potential inherent in the other. The empathic quality to which existentialists aim is an ontological encounter between two individuals, an encounter that is unique, paradoxical, and not technical, based on experience rather than on insight and analysis.

Presence

Presence is aimed at understanding the other from a position of deep willingness to participate (Schneider, 2015). For Bugental (1978), "*presence* is the quality of being in a situation in which one intends to be aware and as participative as one is able to be at that time and in those circumstances. Presence is carried into effect through mobilization of one's inner (toward subjective experiencing) and outer (toward the situation and the other person/s in it) sensitivities" (p. 36). Bugental elaborated by stating that being a unique other and a unique social worker is to be each, in one's unique being in the world and one's own existential situation. Such otherness is a challenge for social workers, who must ascertain their uniqueness to allow the client to participate as a unique person. May (1979) elaborated on this challenge stating that "to be able to sit in a real relationship with another human being who is going through profound anxiety or guilt, or the experience of imminent tragedy tries the best of the humanity in all of us. Therefore, I emphasize the importance of the 'encounter' and use the word rather than 'relationships'" (p. 108). The social worker must choose the extent of immersion in the existential meanings arising from the encounter with the other, and from their existential situation, including the professional, ethical, and interpersonal aspects. The presence involves coming to terms with basic dilemmas of authenticity, compassion, freedom, and so on. Presence emerges differently in various social situations. Thus, presence in prisons is different from that in psychiatric wards or in situations of removal of a child from home and encounters with battered women or batterers.

Mutuality

Mutuality is a critical quality in existential relationships. Edelstein (2015) emphasized the difference between mutuality and hierarchy. Intervention based on hierarchy focuses on the perception of the therapist as an authority and expert figure, relying on theories and diagnostic statements in the intervention. In mutuality, the relationship between the therapist and the client is described by Yalom's metaphor of "fellow travelers" (2002), in other words, a joint human journey (Bugental, 1978). Basic to such a journey is the existential social worker's effort to eschew the position of "the expert" and tolerate the uncertainty alongside the client (Spinelli, 1997). Such an attitude makes possible greater openness to the client's statements.

Mutuality is not to be confused with equality. Buber emphasized that the client comes to the therapist for help and therefore cannot perceive the therapist as a holistic human being, but rather as one in a helper's role. Clients tend to present a one-sided view, focusing on themselves, with no mutuality involved. By contrast, the therapist is expected to see the client and her own view simultaneously. Buber was not deterred by the lack of symmetry in relationships, but rather regarded the gap and the distance as conditions for the emergence of future mutuality. This complexity can also be understood based on Sartre's approach to the view of the other. As noted previously, the other is the key source for knowing the self. The other can transform to "petrify" the "me" to the extent that my ability to break free goes through immobilizing the other (Mui, 2020). The professional's responsibility in the relationship is to liberate the self-petrification and petrification toward the client. Blom (2002) wrote that "The social worker can only experience the client as a subject when the client regards the social worker as an object" (p. 283). The social worker must go through the other to become aware of oneself and to enable the other to become capable of acknowledging the other (the social worker) as subject. The client cannot become *a priori* subject in the relationship. Relationships cannot be abstractly mutual. Rather, mutuality is established through the social worker's pointed effort. Reflecting Buber's perspective, Friedman (1985) wrote: "Only if the therapist discovers the 'otherness' of the client will he or she discover his or her own real limits and what is needed to help the client" (p. 6). This is the turning point in the movement toward mutuality, in which the client chooses to be responsive.

Transference and countertransference

The uniqueness of the existential concept of relating to each other according to the subject-subject attitude as expressed in empathy, presence, and mutuality is illustrated by the concepts of transference and countertransference. The existential ideal of relationships is viewed as real and not based on transference. Yalom viewed transference as giving relationships an "as if" character (1980), in contrast to the existential view of "here and now" real relationships contrasted to the perception that early object relations determine the therapeutic relationship (Schneider, 2007). Cohn (1997) maintained that relatedness is an inevitable part of human relations in the here and now: "The client's as well as the therapist's experience of each other will, of course, also be informed by previous experiences of significant persons, but this does not make the client-therapist experience any less real, though it may make it less transparent and thus in need of clarification" (p. 33). It follows that clients make their own judgments, which are worthy of respect and need not be transformed into any reflection of the past. To use Buber's formulation, relationships do not follow a systematic I-Thou pattern *a priori*. Rather, they are unique to each individual and interpersonal encounter; therefore, countertransference is in contrast with how relationships between clients and workers evolve. As noted, relationships start by recognizing the inability of having a dialogue, recognizing the estrangement and alienation. The fundamental struggle is around realness. Social workers face the challenge of being for themselves and for the other. They experience the self as facing anxiety, responsibility, and the totality of existential topics; therefore, they do not fear inter-subjectivity. Clients share something real, which is common to the interacting dyad. In the existential approach, the relationship is freed from transference and countertransference, as well as from viewing behaviors as confrontations between two subjects in a given situation.

Relationship toward the other as moral responsibility

The meaning of the relationship toward the other is expressed in two moral dictums suggested by Levinas: total respect for the otherness and uniqueness of the other, and infinite responsibility that such otherness demands from the social worker facing the suffering individual (Gantt, 2000). The responsibility toward the other remains in all circumstances infinite and transcendental, and the social worker owes this responsible attitude to the relationship with his client. Gantt (2000) noted that "only when psychotherapy comes to admit this ethical priority, to take on itself the requirements of ethical obligation, will it become truly 'therapeutic' in the fullest and richest sense of that word" (p. 22). The space of suffering brought to therapy by the other creates a touching echo in the social worker's human space: "The human dilemmas expressed in the therapeutic encounter have as much relevance to the therapist as to the client" (van Deurzen, 2002, p. 193). The ethical responsibility involved in such a professional attitude is that the social worker does not act to fix the problem but rather engages another human being struggling with existential issues (Yalom, 1980). By assuming such an attitude, resistance becomes a means of building existential meaning. Heery and Bugenthal (2005) wrote that "Resistances are at the core of our construct of self-and-world; the ways we implicitly define ourselves and our conception of the nature of the world within which we live" (p. 256); therefore, "Resistances are not to be thrown away for they are essential for human life . . . necessary to hold our subjective world together. The question is whether the resistance is truly *serving* the individual. The answer to this question is likely to be disclosed through 'the inner searching of the client rather than the opinion of the psychotherapist or the supervisor of the psychotherapist'" (p. 256). The critical point stems from the ethical recognition that we cannot evade difficulties and misunderstandings arising from the temptation to explain. Rather, one needs to view the gaps, conflicts, and resistance as possibilities for the emergence of I-Thou moments. This is summarized by Friedman (2008) as "the essential element of human existence in which we relate to others in their uniqueness and otherness and not just as the content of our experience" (p. 300).

The challenge of authenticity

Being an existential social worker means constructing professional relationships based on authenticity. Several meanings are known for this term: honesty, realness, and transparency. It means renouncing concealment and masks, not hiding diagnoses, telling the truth straightforwardly, without hiding behind the façade of professionalism, without claiming non-existent knowledge, without refusing to answer questions and addressing doubts, and without denying that the existential dilemmas touch the therapist no less than the client (Yalom, 2008). The social worker invites the client to participate in acknowledging intersubjective mutuality. There is a need to recognize that the individual depends on the other and that intersubjectivity is born from relationships. Authentic participation is a choice.

Authenticity starts at the beginning of the professional relationship in honest clarification of existential intervention, as stated by Iacovou and Weixel-Dixon (2015): "It is the responsibility of the therapist to be explicit about what they are offering in therapy" (p. 89), what are the goals, what values and worldview underlie the intervention, and what methods will be used. An instructive example of what to say to the client can be found in Sommers-Flanagan and Sommers-Flanagan's (2012) formulation of informed consent from the existential perspective: "Our purpose together is to help you face and embrace all of life, rather than running from it. Therefore, much of what we do together will be a real, authentic, mini-life experience wherein you confront the challenges of life and existence within the relatively safe confines of the therapy office. We will use therapy for practicing life rather than for avoiding life." This statement conveys the sincere message of existential intervention. Social workers direct themselves to immerse themselves in the situation of the other. They know that a specific client has a specific authenticity. In Buber's conceptualization, only confirming the authenticity of the other opens up possibilities for an I-Thou relationship.

A condition for authenticity is the demand to eliminate many actions performed as part of the professional script. This elimination produces anxiety. Social workers do not give in to the demands of professional life, not even when they face unclear options vis-à-vis the absurdity of the situation. The recognition of the social worker lies in the power inherent in the creation of authentic meaning for the relationship. In Buber's terms, the social worker recognizes the struggle between seeing and being, and chooses being. Seeing means that the therapist is busy with how the relationship will look, how it will be perceived by the other, and what impression the therapist wants to leave behind for the other. Such a situation establishes images of relationships rather than relationships in the authentic sense. In *being* relationships, the quality of the communication goes full circle around the shared existence, from a position of conserving the uniqueness of every individual.

The other dimension of an authentic relationship has to do with challenging the other, which implies the commitment to speak the truth with the client. This is paradoxical, as it evokes threat but at the same time conveys the belief of the professional in the other's ability to face one's anxieties and transform oneself (Heery & Bugenthal, 2005). The strength of the relationship (the therapeutic alliance) is expressed in the strength of the truth, particularly in moments of existential confrontations. In these situations, the worker doubts the assumptions of the client and directs attention to domains of life situations that are neglected by the individual, who denies, distorts, and even cheats. Authenticity in relationships constitutes a power that stands against forgery, dishonesty, and the manipulations that the individual experiences and uses with others. The more the relationship is based on authenticity, the more the lack of authenticity is revealed, as is the anxiety concerning the loss of existential paths constructed by the individual to achieve adaptation.

One cannot deal with authenticity without addressing the issue of self-disclosure of the therapist. Existentialists consider self-disclosure an important value in constructing authentic relationships, but every self-disclosure must be examined according to the needs of the intervention. The measure of authenticity in self-disclosure was formulated by Spinelli (2007): "*Does this disclosure remain within the overriding aim of seeking to bring into focus and reveal the implicit dispositional stances of the client's worldview that maintain his or her sedimentations and dissociations?*" (p. 161).

Case illustration

The following case example illustrates the various aspects of existential relationships.

Galit, single, 45 years old, physically disabled, in a wheelchair, arrived for a period of rehabilitation at a nursing home following surgery for intestinal occlusion. Given her physical condition and the lack of alternatives, this program was the only possibility suggested to her by the welfare services. Galit refused to participate in the activities of the old people, refused to provide consent for the staff to access her file, which prevented social services from using any information on her other than what she personally provided. Galit locked herself in her room and was unwilling to be supervised by the medical staff. She was unwilling to accept any food from the nursing home, and said that she follows a strict vegetarian diet. She agreed to brief conversations with the social worker, and stated repeatedly that "she has endless problems" and that she "underwent terrible and cruel events in her life." After a short time, Galit demanded that the social worker stop coming to her room and agreed to communicate only by phone. She justified this by saying that she could not concentrate on the things she wanted to do if she knew that at any moment someone was free to interfere with her.

The first task of the existential social worker was to attempt to understand the being in the world of Galit. The social worker was challenged to understand a client who blocked all information about herself, refused to cooperate on anything, and whose self-defeating ways were already established by the staff at the nursing home. This challenge was further exacerbated when Galit informally told the social worker that she suffered from borderline personality disorder and was hospitalized in the past in a mental institution because of self-harming behaviors. The social worker knew from her file that Galit was of above-average intelligence, had graduated from an elite high school, and had a university degree in the social sciences. After graduation, she remained mostly locked up in her parent's residence. The social worker also found out that Galit's relationships with her father were tense, and that the police had been called several times because of screaming in the house. Subsequently, the mother rented small apartments for Galit, far from home. Galit mentioned that she had moved over the years about 50 times.

The social worker decided to continue the relationship over the phone, as Galit requested. She expected to get to know Galit despite the limitations, the diagnosis, and the pressures from other members of the staff in the nursing home. She knew that she needed to base her knowledge of Galit on intersubjectivity rather than on the information provided by others, and on Galit's overt behavior. She decided to fight the tendency to use diagnostic labels toward her, which would only impair her empathy. She decided to be present for her and to accept her subjectivity. One of the manifestations of this decision was to serve as a bridge between the medical and nursing staff and Galit by describing Galit's inner experience to the staff, and describing her own actions and efforts in the mediation process to Galit. The relationship began on the phone, but the conversations became increasingly intense and longer, as Galit shared more and more of her difficulties. Galit began to initiate the calls and called the social worker daily. After several weeks of this pattern, she asked the social worker to come to her room.

Galit told the worker that from early on in her life, she liked being alone and isolated. She said that she does not like relationships with people and wants to keep her distance as much as possible. After several months, the social worker asked Galit how she feels about her presence in her room. The answer which came was:" There are souls I hate, and I don't want any closeness with them; on the other hand, I feel that there are good souls who generally will do no harm to me, and you are one of them." Galit said that the encounter with the social worker was safe and produced understanding. The client shared more and more intimate information with the social worker, and revealed that over the years she experienced abuse from her father and brother, and described humiliations inflicted by the father on her mother. Her mother had died three years earlier from cancer. She had been the only person close to Galit, and since her passing Galit met no one else who could understand her. Galit described life-toward-death as a journey, and said that since her mother went on the journey, there was no one who could understand her. She believed that no one could understand another person's experience unless she experienced the same events with the same intensity and in the same manner. She concluded that there was no chance people could understand each other, and therefore there was no reason to share feelings. Along the same lines, she perceived professionals as agents who can provide technical help, but that one was better off staying away from them emotionally, to avoid "being left with a broken heart, exposed, and broken." She viewed herself as a refugee running from place to place to survive and defend herself by being aggressive and by striking back.

The welfare agency in Galit's area of residence contacted the social worker from the nursing home to suggest a rehabilitation package for Galit. Galit refused, and in the absence of alternative solutions, it was decided to refer her to a psychiatrist to assess her competence, with the possibility of mandatory hospitalization in mind. The psychiatrist visited Galit at the nursing home and in her room. Galit described to the social worker the encounter with the psychiatrist, saying that "the monster came to my room, she behaved with much cruelty." The psychiatrist attempted to obtain personal details, which Galit was unwilling to share with her. Unlike the social worker, who was willing to listen to Galit, the psychiatrist approached her with the attitude that Galit was sick and problematic.

One of the threads in the relationship had to do with the fact that Galit asked the social worker personal questions, including where she lived, what were her preferences, does she like where she lived, where did her parents live, and various existential issues such as faith, meaning in life, and the social worker's attempts to deal with difficult life events. To most of these questions, the social worker answered authentically. She felt that she could see Galit as a complete human being, and their relationship was one between two subjects encountering each other, rather than one between therapist and client. Such an understanding of Galit provided safety to the social worker when questioned about her personal life and when she was listening to details of Galit's life. She often chose to give up her interpretation of what was being said, thereby confirming the relationship between them, which enabled Galit's subjectivity together with the expectation of sharing and accepting her subjectivity as a social worker.

This intersubjectivity makes it possible to focus on the issue of choice in Galit's life. The social worker points out to Galit the ways in which difficult life events are responsible for her sense of having no choice in the present. Galit presents herself in a passive position, where things in her life are beyond her control. This results in continual deterioration triggered by detachment and alienation. The social worker feels that there is a common intersubjective ground that developed between them, which makes it possible to raise such difficult issues. She and Galit feel safe enough to deal with these issues on a basis of mutuality, in the context of an authentic dialogue. The social worker points out that Galit's meeting with the psychiatrist made her face a choice in how to relate to another being, similarly to her relationship with the social worker. The social worker stresses the fact that Galit can continue with her past negative experiences, being avoidant and hostile. Alternatively, she could become active, initiate, and share based on the belief that her actions have a constructive potential. Galit answered that this is a difficult task, which seemed impossible to her. She mentioned that in the past she has heard a rabbi saying that "If God sends you a difficult situation, He wants to punish you, and you need to accept it." The social worker responded that in her view, when such events take place, God wants to leave it up to the person how to act. The meaning of the life event remains in your hand: you can allow yourself to be broken, or you can grow from it.

A month after the event described here, Galit was asked to undergo psychiatric testing. She came to the meeting and explained to the psychiatrist at the hospital her situation directly and authentically. She shared with the psychiatrist how she would want to live and what was acceptable for her. Following her self-presentation, Galit was not hospitalized and returned to the nursing home. This was a surprise to the social worker because it marked the first time that Galit expressed her view and made her voice heard before a professional person. In existential terms, Galit understood the choices available to her and exercised her choice. This was in sharp contrast with previous occasions when she could have exercised her choice but evaded it. In her discussions with the social worker, she pointed out that it was the first time she was able to carry out this difficult and complex task. She began to reexamine her lack of collaboration with the staff at the nursing home and defined it as unnecessary suffering.

We believe that the process described here illustrates the essence of the relationship in existential intervention. First, relationships are tied to the existential content and structure as well as to changes in the professional intervention and its outcomes. Galit experienced the willingness to examine choices considering a relationship. The knowledge that another was available to focus on the depth of the relationship, in the here and now, despite negative emotions such as hostility and rejection, was a new source of motivation for change. Second, the encounter between the social worker and Galit was based on the realness and authenticity of the relationship, combining the professional and the personal. Third, empathy and respect for the version of the client's being in the world is central. Fourth, the mutuality in the I-Thou relationship helps focus on existential issues rather than on diagnostic categories, transference, and countertransference. The expected outcome is mutuality between two beings in the social worker's and Galit's world. Fifth, in existential therapy, the relationship with the other is a moral responsibility. The social worker was willing to limit herself and accept Galit's way of establishing relationships. The limitation imposed on the professional self led to an expansion of her intersubjective side, which in turn, seems to have affected Galit's being in the world.

We can summarize this chapter by concluding that the total respect for the otherness and uniqueness of the other, and the infinite responsibility to achieve it, are the challenges of the professional social worker, extending beyond the appearances of the process.

Epilogue
Life after the book

Every book has a life of its own after the reader is done with it. This is the result of the meaning constructed by the reader from the encounter with the book, in the reader's experience of being in the world. This book is meant to provide readers with an opportunity to participate in the lives of the people who come to seek their professional advice and intervention, out of a sense of commitment to their welfare and growth. The book further seeks to provide an understanding of the existential issues underlying the pain, anxiety, and misery of human existence, together with hope, courage, and coping. We attempted to shed light on the existential themes and questions present in the professional and personal lives of people. Our intention was to present these while attempting to seek authentic relationships. These, we hope, will enhance the understanding of clients and motivate them to change.

Overall, we sought to identify three goals in intervention. The first is to foster self-understanding of the experience of being in the world. This develops the ability and motivation to reflect on existential themes affecting one's life narrative in a given context, at a certain moment in time, together with significant others. All these are expected to be achieved despite the anxiety involved.

The second goal is to encourage the other (the client) to accept oneself as a choosing and acting person, struggling against the sense of lack of choice and of determinism. Individuals must acknowledge the broad range of possibilities beyond the existing limitations and tragic blockages, working from a sense of recognizing freedom as a basic attitude toward life circumstances, and of ongoing intentionality and involvement in life, being responsible for their own and others' lives. Such freedom goes along with the inevitability of the heavy burden of life, within the limitations of power. There is recognition that choices must be made, and it is unclear which ones are right and which ones are wrong.

The third goal is to heal and reconstruct meaning in meaningless situations, arising from unclear answers to the question of who one is. Following failure in relationships to assign meaning, and the subsequent

DOI: 10.4324/9781003322085-11

disappointments arising from individual behaviors of others and from specific life circumstances, healing is needed. People experience despair in situations of this type, and we hope to empower and give hope through authentic self-search, which precludes taken-for-grantedness. This involves clarity and a worldview that makes possible transcendence and the actualization of meaning.

We started out with the intent to write the ultimate book that furnishes the final answer, disperses professional doubts and conflicts, and provides an all-out prescription of how to intervene existentially. In the final analysis, we finished the book with the recognition that this is merely a starting point rather than the end of the road. As existence itself, every endpoint is a beginning based on the recognition that there is always a lack, something is missing. In such experiences, the individual is expected to create and recreate meaning. You, the esteemed reader, are left with the expectation to reflect and redo, to construct your own way of doing existential work. The book is nothing more than a guide to searching for answers that you construct, and occasionally, experience finding them. Our aim was to help construct a theoretical home.

In the life after the book, you are invited to decide what you wish to take away from it. This may help you gain more clarity in deciding what you need to actualize and change in your professional perceptions. This is a continuous and challenging process of struggle between anxiety and passion: anxiety from the expectations of existential theory to reflect and choose. Take, for example, the recognition of one's freedom to construct a life project of being-a-social-worker. This is associated with passion to actualize one's freedom and choice, together with the responsibility involved. We hope that we were able to awaken in the readers such "passion for the sea" as Antoine de Saint-Exupéry described. Whether we succeeded or not is for you to decide.

We started the book by quoting the last line of Camus' essay, *The Myth of Sisyphus*. It is only fitting to end it by quoting the first line of that essay: "There is only one really serious philosophical question, and that is suicide." In his essay, Camus demonstrates the attitude toward life that deters suicide. His main concern is to outline paths for going through life in a way that makes it worth living despite its meaningless.

In a series of declarative sentences, Dylan Thomas depicts the anguish at the end of life of those who in bad faith failed to make the necessary choices when offered. Wise men who failed to make courageous choices "do not go gentle" to their death. Good men who timidly withdrew from acting "rage against the dying light." The respectable and the non-conformist alike, who failed to comprehend and assume responsibility for being, rage against death when their hour is approaching. In the last stanza, the same *declarative* words become *imperatives*, as Thomas addresses his father: "Do not!" As long as there is breath, it is not too late to choose, and if need be, to rebel. Thomas beseeches his father, even at the extreme end of life, to take action, any action:

> And you, my father, there on the sad height,
> Curse, bless, me now with your fierce tears, I pray.
> Do not go gentle into that good night.
> Rage, rage against the dying of the light.

References

Adams, M. (2016). Existential therapy as a skill-learning process. *Existential Analysis, 27*, 58–69.

Adams, M. (2018). *An existential approach to human developmental: Philosophical and therapeutic perspectives*. Palgrave Macmillan.

Améry, J. (1994). *On aging: Revolt and resignation* (J. D. Barlow, Trans.). Indiana University Press.

Barry, V. (2007). *Philosophical thinking about death and dying*. Thompson/Wadsworth.

Batthyany, A., & Russo-Netzer, P. (Eds.). (2014). *Meaning in positive and existential psychology*. Springer.

Baxter, L. A. (2004). Relationships and dialogues. *Personal Relationships, 11*, 1–22.

Blom, B. (2002). The social worker-client relationship: A Sartrean approach. *European Journal of Social Work, 5*, 277–285.

Boss, M. (1963). *Psychoanalysis and daseinanalysis*. Basic Books.

Bruner, J. (1990). *Acts of meaning*. Harvard University Press.

Buben, A. (2015). An attempt at clarifying being-towards-death. In H. Pedersen & M. Altman (Eds.), *Horizons of authenticity in phenomenology, existentialism, and moral psychology: Essays in honor of Charles Guignon* (pp. 201–217). Springer.

Buber, M. (2000). *I and Thou* (G. Smith, Trans.). Scribner Classics. (Original work published 1923)

Bugental, J. F. T. (1978). *Psychotherapy and process: The foundation of an existential-humanistic approach*. McGraw-Hill.

Calhoun, L. G., & Tedeschi, R. G. (1999). *Facilitating posttraumatic growth: A clinician's guide*. Lawrence Erlbaum.

Camus, A. (1955). *The Sisyphus and other essays* (J. O'Brien, Trans.). Vintage Books. (Original work published 1942)

Carel, H. (2008). *Illness: The cry of the flesh*. Acumen.

Carel, H. (2016). *Phenomenology of illness*. Oxford University Press.

Chekhov, A. (1921). *Note book of Anton Chekhov* (S. S. Koteliansky & L. Woolf, Trans.). B. W. Huebsch.

Cohn, H. W. (1997). *Existential thought and therapeutic practice: An introduction to existential psychotherapy*. SAGE.

Cooper, M. (1990). *Existentialism: A reconstruction*. Basil Blackwell.

Cooper, M. (2008). *Essential research findings in counseling and psychotherapy.* SAGE.

Cox, G. (2009). *How to be an existentialist or how to get real, get a grip and stop making excuses.* Continuum.

Daigle, C. (2010). *Jean-Paul Sartre.* Routledge.

Daigle, C. (2011). The ethics of authenticity. In J. Webber (Ed.), *Reading Sartre: On phenomenology and existentialism* (pp. 1–14). Routledge.

Denzin, N. K. (1984). Toward phenomenology of domestic, family violence. *American Journal of Sociology, 90,* 483–513.

DuBose, T. (2016). Out, out, brief candle? The meaning of meaninglessness. In P. Russo-Netzer, S. E. Schulenberg, & A. Batthyany (Eds.), *Clinical perspectives on meaning* (pp. 283–295). Springer.

Edelstein, B. (2015). Frames, attitudes, and skills of an existential-humanistic psychotherapist. In K. J. Schneider, J. Fraser Pierson & J. E. T. Bugental (Eds.), *The handbook of humanistic psychology* (second edition) (pp. 435–450). Sage.

Egan, G., & Reese, R. J. (2019). *The skilled helper: A problem-management & opportunity-development approach to helping* (7th ed.). Cengage.

Ellenberger, H. F. (1958). A clinical introduction to psychiatric phenomenology and existential analysis. In R. May, E. Angel, & H. E. Ellenberger (Eds.), *Existence: A new dimension in psychiatry and psychology* (pp. 37–91). Basic Books.

Eshleman, M. C. (2011). What is it like to be free? In J. Webber (Ed.), *Reading Sartre: On phenomenology and existentialism* (pp. 31–47). Routledge.

Fischer, W. (1970). The faces of anxiety. *Journal of Phenomenological Psychology, 1,* 31–49.

Frankl, V. F. (1969). *Man's search for meaning: An introduction to logotherapy* (I. Lasch, Trans.). Beacon Press. (Original work published 1946)

Frankl, V. F. (1988). *The will to meaning: Foundations and application of Logotherapy* (Expanded ed.). Penguin Books. (Original work published 1969)

Friedman, M. S. (1985). *The healing dialogue in psychotherapy.* Northvale, NJ: Jason Aronson.

Friedman, M. S. (2002). *Martin Buber: The life of dialogue.* Routledge.

Friedman, M. S. (2008). Buber and dialogical therapy: Healing through meeting. *The Humanistic Psychologist, 36,* 298–315.

Gantt, E. E. (2000). Levinas, psychotherapy, and the ethics of suffering. *Journal of Humanistic Psychology, 40,* 9–28.

Goldie, P. (2014). *The mess inside: Narrative, emotion, & the mind.* Oxford University Press.

Golomb, J. (1995). *In search of authenticity: From Kierkegaard to Camus.* Routledge.

Griffiths, M. (2017). *The challenge of existential social work practice.* Macmillan Education/Palgrave.

Heery, M., & Bugenthal, J. F. T. (2005). Meaning and transformation. In E. van Deurzen & C. Arnold-Baker (Eds.), *Existential perspectives on human issues: A handbook for therapeutic practice* (pp. 253–264). Palgrave Macmillan.

Heidegger, M. (1996). *Being and time: A translation of Sein und Zeit* (J. Stambaugh, Trans.). State University of New York Press. (Original work published 1927)

Hill, C. E. (2004). *Helping skills: Facilitating exploration, insight, and action* (2nd ed.). American Psychological Association.

Hill, C. E. (2018). *Meaning in life: A therapist's guide.* American Psychological Association.

Hoffman, P. (1986). *Doubt, time, violence.* The University of Chicago Press.

Iacovou, S., & Weixel-Dixon, K. (2015). *Existential therapy; 100 key points and techniques.* Routledge.

Jaspers, J. (1967). *The nature of psychotherapy: A critical appraisal* (J. Hoening & M. W. Hamilton, Trans.). The University of Chicago Press.

Josselson, R., & Hopkins, B. (2015). Narrative psychology and life stories. In J. Martin, J. Sugarman, & K. L. Slaney (Eds.), *The Wiley handbook of theoretical and philosophical psychology: Methods, approaches, and new directions* (pp. 219–233). Chichester: Wiley Blackwell.

Koenig, T. R. (1997). *Existentialism and human existence: An account of five major philosophers.* Krieger.

Krill, D. (1996). Existential social work. In F. J. Turner (Ed.), *Social work treatment: Interlocking theoretical approaches* (pp. 250–281). The Free Press.

Kunz, G. (2002). Simplicity, humility, patience. In E. E. Gantt & R. N. Williams (Eds.), *Psychology of the other: Levinas, ethics and the practice of psychology* (pp. 118–142). Duquesne University Press.

Laing, R. D. (1960). *The divided self: An existential study in sanity and madness.* Penguin.

Lakoff, G., & Johnson, M. (1980). *Metaphors we live by.* The University of Chicago Press.

Landau, I. (2017). *Finding meaning in an imperfect world.* Oxford University Press.

Large, W. (2015). *Levinas' 'totality and infinity'.* Bloomsbury.

Leontiev, D. A. (2013). Personal meaning: A challenge for psychology. *The Journal of Positive Psychology, 8,* 459–470.

Levi, Z. (2008). *Reflection on death—in philosophy and in Jewish thought.* Resling (In Hebrew).

Levinas, E. (1969). *Totality and infinity: An essay on exteriority* (A. Lingis, Trans.). Duquesne University Press. (Original work published 1961)

Levinas, E. (1987). *Time and the other and additional essays* (R. A. Cohen, Trans.). Duquesne University Press. (Original work published 1947)

Linde, C. (1993). *Life stories.* Oxford.

Luper, S. (2009). *The philosophy of death.* Cambridge University Press.

Lurie, Y. (2006). *Tracking the meaning of life: A philosophical journey.* University of Missouri Press.

Maddi, S. R. (2012). Creating meaning through making decisions. In P. T. P. Wong (Ed.), *The human quest for meaning* (2nd ed., pp. 57–80). Routledge.

Martin, D. J., Garske, J. P., & Davis, M. K. (2000). Relation of the therapuetic alliance with outcome and other variables: A meta-analytic review. *Journal of Consulting and Clinical Psychology, 68,* 438–450.

May, R. (1958). Contributions of existential psychotherapy. In R. May, E. Angel, & H. E. Ellenberger (Eds.), *Existence: A new dimension in psychiatry and psychology* (pp. 37–92). Basic Books.

May, R. (1979). *Psychology and the human dilemma.* W. W. Norton.

May, R. (1983). *The discovery of being: Writings in existential psychology.* W. W. Norton.

May, R., & Yalom, I. D. (1995). Existential psychotherapy. In R. J. Corsini & D. Wedding (Eds.), *Current psychotherapies* (pp. 262–292). F.E. Peacock.

May, R., & Yalom. I. (2000). Existential psychotherapy. In R. J. Corsini & D. Wedding (Eds.), *Current psychotherapies* (pp. 273–302). F. E. Peacock.

McAdams, D. P. (1996). *The stories we live by: Personal myths and making the self.* William Morrow.

Merleau-Ponty, M. (2012). *Phenomenology of perception* (D. A. Landes, Trans.). Routledge. (Original work published 1945)

Miron, R. (2012). *Karl Jaspers: From selfhood to being.* Editions Rodopi.

Morgan, M. L. (2011). *The Cambridge introduction to Emmanuel Levinas.* Cambridge University Press.

Moustakas, C. (1995). *Being-in, being-for, being with.* Jason Aronson.

Mui, C. L. (2020). Intersubjectivity and "the look". In M. C. Eshleman & C. L. Mui (Eds.), *The Sartrean mind* (pp. 212–224). Routledge.

Mulhall, S. (1996). *Heidegger and being and time.* Routledge.

Nagel, T. (1979). *Mortal questions.* Cambridge University Press.

Neimeyer, R. A. (2000). Narrative disruptions in the construction of the self. In R. A. Neimeyer & J. D. Raskin (Eds.), *Constructions of disorder: Meaning-making frameworks for psychotherapy* (pp. 207–242). American Psychological Association.

Neimeyer, R. A. (2004). Fostering posttraumatic growth: A narrative elaboration. *Psychological Inquiry, 15,* 53–59.

Orbach, I. (2007). Existentialism and suicide. In A. Tomer, G. T. Eliason, & P. T. P. Wong (Eds.), *Existential and spiritual issues in death attitudes* (pp. 281–316). Lawrence Erlbaum Associates.

Pollard, J. (2005). Authenticity and inauthenticity. In E. van Deurzen & C. Arnold-Baker (Eds.), *Existential perspectives on human issues: A handbook for therapeutic practice* (pp. 171–179). Palgrave Macmillan.

Reynolds, J. (2006). *Understanding existentialism.* Acumen.

Richardson, J. (2012). *Heidegger.* Routledge.

Richert, A. J. (1999). Some thoughts on the integration of narrative and humanistic/existential approaches to psychotherapy. *Journal of Psychotherapy Integration, 9,* 161–184.

Richert, A. J. (2002). The self in narrative therapy: Thoughts from a humanistic/existential perspective. *Journal of Psychotherapy Integration, 12,* 77–104.

Ricoeur, P. (1984). *Time and narrative.* The University of Chicago Press.

Sagi, A. (2018). *Living with the other: The ethic of inner retreat.* Springer.

Saleebey, D. (2006). The strengths approach to practice. In D. Saleebey (Ed.), *The strengths perspective in social work practice* (pp. 3–19). Pearson/Allyn & Bacon.

Saleebey, D. (Ed.). (2009). Power in the people. In D. Saleebey (Ed.), *The strengths perspective in social work practice* (5th ed., pp. 1–23). Pearson/Allyn & Bacon.

Sarbin, T. R. (1986). *Narrative psychology: The storied nature of human conduct.* Praeger.

Sartre, J. P. (1948). *Humanism and existentialism* (P. Mairet, Trans.). Methuen. (Original work published 1946)

Sartre, J. P. (1949). *No exit and three other plays*. Vintage Books.

Sartre, J. P. (1966). *Being and nothingness: An essay on phenomenological ontology* (H. E. Barnes, Trans.). Methuen. (Original work published 1943)

Sartre, J. P. (1969). *Nausea* (L. Alexander, Trans.). New Directions Book. (Original work published 1938)

Scarre, G. (2007). *Death*. McGill-Queen's University Press.

Schechtman, M. (2011). The narrative self. In S. Gallagher (Ed.), *The Oxford handbook of the self* (pp. 394–416). Oxford University Press.

Schlitte, A. (2017). Narrative and place. In B. B. Janz (Ed.), *Place, space and hermeneutics* (pp. 35–48). Springer.

Schneider, K. J. (Ed.). (2007). *Existential-integrative psychotherapy: Guideposts to the core of practice*. Routledge.

Schneider, K. J. (2015). Presence: The core contextual factor of effective psychotherapy. *Existential Analysis*, 2, 304–312.

Sommers-Flanagan, J., & Sommers-Flanagan, R. (2012(. *Counseling and psychotherapy theories in context and practice: Skills, strategies, and techniques* (2nd ed.). Wiley.

Sontag, S. (1990). *Illness and metaphor and aids and its metaphors*. Anchor Books Doubleday.

Spinelli, E. (1989). *The interpreted world: An introduction to phenomenological psychology*. SAGE.

Spinelli, E. (1997). *Tales of un-knowing: Eight stories of existential therapy*. New York University Press.

Spinelli, E. (2007). *Practicing existential psychotherapy: The relational world*. SAGE.

Spinelli, E. (2016). Experiencing change: An existential perspective. In S. E. Schulenberg (Ed.), *Clarifying and furthering existential psychotherapy: Theories, methods, and practices* (pp. 131–143). Springer.

Spinelli, E. (2019). What's so existential about existential therapy? *Existential Analysis: Journal of the Society for Existential Analysis*, 30, 59–79.

Thompson, N. (1992). *Existentialism and social work*. Avebury.

Thompson, N. (2017). *Theorizing practice: A guide to the people professions* (2nd ed.). Macmillan Education/Palgrave.

Tillich, P. (1966). *The courage to be*. Yale University Press. (Original work published 1952)

van Deurzen, E. (2000). *Everyday mysteries: A handbook of existential psychotherapy* (second edition). Sage.

van Deurzen, E. (2002). Existential therapy. In W. Dryden (Ed.), *Handbook of individual therapy* (pp. 179–208). Sage.

van Deurzen, E., & Adams, M. (2011). *Skills in existential counselling & psychotherapy* (2nd ed.). SAGE.

van Deurzen-Smith, E. (1997). *Everyday mysteries: Existential dimensions of psychotherapy*. SAGE.

Vetlesen, A. J. (2009). *A philosophy of pain*. (J. Irons, Trans.). Reaktion Books.

Webber, J. (2009). *The existentialism of Jean-Paul Sartre*. Routledge.

Webber, J. (2011). Bad faith and the other. In J. Webber (Ed.), *Reading Sartre: On phenomenology and existentialism* (pp. 180–194). Routledge.

White, C. J. (2005). *Time and death: Heidegger's analysis of finitude*. Ashgate.

Willis, R. J. (1994). *Transcendence in relationship: Existentialism and psychotherapy*. Ablex Publishing Corporation.

Wong, P. T. P. (2010). Meaning therapy: An integrative and positive existential psychotherapy. *Journal of Contemporary Psychotherapy, 40*, 85–99.

Wong, P. T. P. (2012). Toward a dual-systems model of what makes life worth living. In P. T. P. Wong (Ed.), *The human quest for meaning* (2nd ed., pp. 3–22). Routledge.

Yalom, I. D. (1980). *Existential psychotherapy.* Basic Books.

Yalom, I. D. (2002). *The gist of therapy: An open letter to a new generation of therapists and their clients.* HarperCollins.

Yalom, I. D. (2008). *Staring at the sun: Overcoming the terror of death.* Jossey-Bass.

Yalom, I. D., & Josselson, R. (2011). Existential psychotherapy. In R. J. Corsini & D. Wedding (Eds.), *Current psychotherapies* (9th ed., pp. 310–341). Brooks/Cole.

Zahavi, D. (2011). Shame and the exposed self. In J. Webber (Ed.), *Reading Sartre: On phenomenology and existentialism* (pp. 211–226). Routledge.

Index

For Product Safety Concerns and Information please contact our EU
representative GPSR@taylorandfrancis.com
Taylor & Francis Verlag GmbH, Kaufingerstraße 24, 80331 München, Germany

www.ingramcontent.com/pod-product-compliance
Lightning Source LLC
Chambersburg PA
CBHW050614280326
41932CB00016B/3045